WATER GATE INN

OLD ORIGINAL BOOKBINDER'S

Marshall Field & Company

Win Schuler's

DAVEN HAVEN

PERINO'S

Camellia ROOM

FAMOUS FOODS
from
FAMOUS PLACES

Better Homes and Gardens
FAMOUS FOODS

MEREDITH PRESS, New York, Des Moines

from FAMOUS PLACES

INTRODUCTION

Often an exciting and memorable reward of an interesting trip is the experience of new foods in unusual places. No traveler could really touch down at all our truly good places to eat. When you name one favorite and famous restaurant, friends may recount two they've also enjoyed in that same city. Only on these we visited are we able to pass the best judgment, to report accurately our experiences. We lament the many discriminating ones we've had to leave in the file of our search, but people hunting fine food will find their deserving doors. Each restaurant included is a representative place open to you and to the traveling public. Some are family places, some intimate and some of fabled eminence. With each recipe selected comes the generous permission of the establishment to which it is credited.

The genesis of the title, FAMOUS FOODS FROM FAMOUS PLACES, came from one of the best-read features in Better Homes and Gardens magazine. Its popularity year after year and the letters from readers alerted our foods editors to the joy of exploring show-case restaurants for new flavor combinations, new treatments, and new perfection. The challenge in color, shape, and texture, the succulence and fragility of many foods attracts the most skillful photographers; they have captured on film the very steam from a souffle, the dewy freshness of sun-grown vegetables and fruits.

Under test kitchen scrutiny and with the professional curiosity of our foods editors, the recipes are fail-proof. To bring them to you and to your kitchen, we've adjusted them to family-size proportions. Your attempt to duplicate a recipe may not look as glamorous as it looks in our picture, so dress it up yourself with what you have on hand. A recipe may surprise you on the first trial. Try it again. True, it won't be accompanied by epergnes of beautiful flowers, by wing-borne melodies, and symphonic fountains. It will not be prepared at your table in a handsome bronze chafing dish by a scarlet-coated waiter, but it can bring pleasant memories, can compliment your family and guests and show your ingenuity.

The myth that famous chefs are unwilling to tell you about their creations isn't true. Actually they took pride in telling us about the special recipes we chose. A creative chef may have trouble putting into words the exact way he prepares a gourmet dish. What he does is often in the realm of instinct. Let us also give credit to the sorcery of foods editors of today's magazines, to their growing resourcefulness in food preparation, and to what they've done to make cookery books fascinating and reliable.

Page confines give too little space in which to pay full respect to proud restaurant staffs. We describe the mood of each restaurant, give a few details of its history. The greater space we saved for the recipes themselves. Some were once regional. Of many, the origin has disappeared from history. No man recorded them as Charles Lamb did the famous first roast pig. Romantic and foreign names shouldn't trouble you; their names had a meaning when first offered proudly to some excited person. Remember the first time you were served a steaming baked potato, drizzled first with butter, then topped with a dressing of sour cream and chopped chives? Now it's a menu standard from East to West. Who knows where it originated?

For you who set forth adventuresomely on the pleasure of being served beautifully and of enjoying every eaten morsel, this book should be as entertaining as it is instructive. It's a reminder of pleasant places to which you've been, a touchstone to places to which you may be going. It's also a trusty guide book for satisfying your food quests, and a must for the cook book collector's shelf. In simple measure we say proudly that we have been to every one of the restaurants we've included. We found each place worth going to; we're certain that you would too.

The Editors

CONTENTS

Continued

CONTENTS

NEW YORK

Hotel Pierre

Through the ages man's need for food has wielded great influence on the history of man. In the Pierre Grill, huge murals created by Edgar Miller, an American artist, depict occasions when the partaking of food has been particularly meaningful to our country. The Feast of Montezuma, The Pilgrim's Thanksgiving, at the Governor's Palace in Williamsburg, and Mealtime in Valley Forge represent an integral part of American food traditions.

The Pierre Grill is the most relaxed and informal of the three public dining rooms in the Hotel Pierre. Included on its menu is the offbeat addition of exotic East Indian curries. Curry powder, the predominant spice in curries, is an inspiration from India, where the use of spices is an art which dates from the very beginnings of civilized history. Curry has, in fact, been called the "salt of the East," so prevalent is it in their cookery. The Grill features two curries each day, Chicken Curry (left) plus either lamb, beef, veal, or sea food. The recipes are authentically prepared by two East Indian chefs, and have been highly praised by visitors from India and other "curryphiles."

Enjoying a curry at the Grill is a delightful experience. East Indian boys, dressed in their colorful native costumes, wheel the curry wagon right to your table, and serve you with great ceremony. First, they spoon the bright yellow Saffron Rice onto the warm plate, then top it with the richly flavored Chicken Curry. Since curry calls for condiments, you make your choice from the assortment on the wagon (at left in picture)—white raisins, chopped parsley, grated orange rind, grated fresh coconut, chopped peanuts, chutney, Papadums, and Bombay duck—to complete the meal.

CHICKEN CURRY

½ cup chopped onion
1 clove garlic, minced
¼ cup salad oil
1 medium tomato, chopped
1 small bay leaf
½ teaspoon cinnamon
3 whole cloves
5 cups cubed uncooked chicken (2½ pounds boned)
1½ teaspoons salt
1 tablespoon curry powder
½ teaspoon cumin
½ teaspoon coriander
Dash pepper
Pinch powdered saffron
1½ cups water
¼ cup fresh coconut milk

In large skillet cook onions and garlic in oil till tender but not brown. Add tomato, bay leaf, cinnamon, and cloves; cover and cook 5 minutes. Add chicken cubes; simmer uncovered slowly till juice of chicken has steamed off (about 30 minutes). Stir in salt, curry powder, cumin, coriander, pepper, saffron, and water. Cook slowly for 35 to 40 minutes, or till chicken is tender. Blend in coconut milk. Serve hot over Saffron Rice. Makes 6 to 8 servings.

SAFFRON RICE

Dash powdered saffron
½ cup hot water
¼ cup butter or margarine, melted
1½ cups uncooked rice
¼ cup chopped onion
½ teaspoon salt
2½ cups hot water

Dissolve saffron in ½ cup hot water. Combine the dissolved saffron, butter, rice, onion, salt, and *1 cup* of the water in a 1½-quart casserole. Bake in hot oven (450°) for 20 minutes or till rice is very dry, stirring at the end of 10 minutes. Stir in remaining 1½ cups hot water; cover and return to hot oven for 15 minutes. Uncover and cook 5 minutes longer. Fluff with fork before serving. Makes 8 to 12 servings.

BREAST OF CAPON ISABELLE

6 breasts of capon, boned, skinned, and split lengthwise
2 tablespoons butter or margarine
2½ cups chicken stock

• • •

1 pound tiny noodles
2 tablespoons butter or margarine

• • •

1 pint fresh mushrooms, sliced (about 2 cups sliced)
¼ cup butter or margarine
¼ cup dry white wine
½ teaspoon salt
Dash pepper
2 tablespoons all-purpose flour

• • •

¼ cup butter or margarine
¼ cup all-purpose flour
1 teaspoon salt
Dash pepper
2 cups light cream
3 slightly beaten egg yolks

In a large skillet brown the breasts of capon in 2 tablespoons butter. Add *2 tablespoons* of the chicken stock; cover and cook for 30 minutes or till tender.

Meanwhile, cook the noodles in boiling, salted water. When tender, drain; toss lightly with 2 tablespoons butter; keep hot.

While noodles are cooking, cook the sliced mushrooms in ¼ cup butter with the wine, ½ teaspoon salt, and dash pepper till tender, about 5 minutes; sprinkle with 2 tablespoons flour and stir to blend; keep warm.

Remove the breasts of capon from skillet; keep warm while making sauce. In same skillet, melt ¼ cup butter; blend in ¼ cup flour, 1 teaspoon salt and dash pepper. Add remaining chicken stock and the light cream all at once; cook, stirring constantly, until mixture comes to boiling. Remove from heat; stir a little hot mixture into egg yolks; return to hot mixture. Then continue cooking, stirring constantly, just till mixture comes to boiling. Remove from heat.

To serve, place breasts of capon on bed of hot buttered noodles; top with the mushroom mixture and then pour the cream sauce over all. Makes 8 to 12 servings.

NEW YORK

Café Chauveron

Posh Cafe Chauveron in New York City's East Fifties specializes in "la cuisine francaise pour les gourmets." French as Proprietor Mr. Roger Chauveron's background, this restaurant is a favorite habitat for the "Who's Who" of the financial and retailing world—among other New Yorkers.

Through the window between dining room and kitchen, you can see a gleaming array of copper pans from France, which seem to promise long-simmered sauces as are found in French cookery books, and melding of flavors par excellence. Roast Duckling with Oranges is no exception to the promises. It's a delectable French specialty that lives up to every expectation in goodness and flavor.

ROAST DUCKLING WITH ORANGES

2 ducklings, each 4 to 5 pounds ready-to-cook weight
Salt
3 medium oranges
2 tablespoons sugar
2 teaspoons vinegar
2 cups thick veal stock or canned condensed beef broth
1½ tablespoons lemon juice
3 teaspoons arrowroot starch
½ cup sweet sherry
⅓ cup orange liqueur

Clean ducklings and pat dry. Rub inside of ducks with salt; skewer opening and lace shut. Prick skin well all over to allow fat to escape. Roast on a rack in shallow pan in hot oven (400°) about 1½ hours or till meaty part of leg feels tender when pressed (use paper towel). Spoon off fat occasionally. While ducks roast, shave peel from *2 of the* oranges with vegetable parer and cut in julienne strips; squeeze juice from *all 3* oranges. Set peel and juice aside.

When ducks are done, place on heated platter and keep hot while making ***Orange Sauce:*** Remove drippings from roasting pan and skim off fat; set pan juices aside. Caramelize the sugar with vinegar in roasting pan; add reserved pan juices, veal stock, orange juice and peel, and lemon juice. Cook sauce rapidly to reduce by *half*. Blend arrowroot and sherry; gradually stir into sauce; cook, *stirring*, 6 to 8 minutes or till thick and clear—don't let bubble. Add orange liqueur just before serving.

To serve, garnish ducklings with orange sections, if desired. Pass hot Orange Sauce. Makes 8 servings.

NEW YORK

Tower Suite

In this city of sophistication, Tower Suite serves the ultimate—a superb seven course meal on the 48th floor of New York's Time & Life Building. Rising high on the dessert cart at left is a very rich hazelnut and maple flavored Sugarbush Bombe among a variety of fruits, cheeses, and pastries. In the background is an elegant loaf of Chocolate Whipped Cream Cake.

CHOCOLATE WHIPPED CREAM CAKE

3 1-ounce squares semisweet chocolate
4 ounces (½ cup) almond paste, crumbled
¼ cup milk
2 eggs
2 egg yolks
½ cup sifted all-purpose flour
¼ cup almonds, toasted and ground
¼ cup semisweet chocolate pieces
2 egg whites
¼ cup sugar

• • •

¾ cup semisweet chocolate pieces
½ cup evaporated milk

• • •

1 cup whipping cream
1 tablespoon sugar
Whole toasted almonds
Confectioners' sugar

Combine chocolate squares, almond paste, and milk. Cook and stir till melted; cool. Beat eggs and egg yolks till foamy; gradually blend in chocolate mixture. Stir in flour, almonds, and ¼ cup chocolate pieces. Beat egg whites till frothy; gradually add sugar, beating to stiff peaks. Gently fold egg whites into chocolate mixture till well blended. Turn into a greased and floured 10¼x3⅝x-2⅝-inch loaf pan. Bake at 350° for 40 minutes. Cool; split into 2 layers.

Combine ¾ cup chocolate pieces and evaporated milk; cook and stir over low heat till smooth and thickened, about 3 to 5 minutes. Cool and spread on tops and sides of both layers of cake. Beat whipping cream and 1 tablespoon sugar together till stiff. Spread on one glazed layer; gently top with the second layer. If desired trim with whole toasted almonds; dust lightly with confectioners' sugar. Makes 10 to 12 servings.

ROAST DUCKLING WITH POMEGRANATE

1 4-pound ready-to-cook duckling
¾ cup chopped onion
½ cup chopped carrot
½ cup chopped celery
2 tablespoons cooking oil
1¼ cups chicken broth
¾ cup grenadine syrup
1 tablespoon butter or margarine
1 tablespoon sugar
1 tablespoon *each* lemon and lime juice
1 teaspoon cornstarch
¼ cup Grand Marnier

Prick duckling to allow fat to escape; truss. Roast on rack in 375° oven for 1½ hours; then in 425° oven for 15 minutes or till golden brown and tender. Meanwhile make sauce: In a skillet brown giblets, neck, wing tips, and vegetables in hot oil. Add broth; cover and simmer 1 hour. Strain. Add ½ *cup* of the grenadine syrup; reduce sauce to ½. In saucepan melt butter; blend in sugar and cook till brown. Add citrus juices and remaining ¼ cup grenadine. Stir in broth mixture. Remove duckling from pan; keep hot. Skim off fat from pan; add remaining meat juices to sauce. Blend cornstarch with Grand Marnier; add to sauce. Cook and stir 2 to 3 minutes. (Makes about 1½ cups sauce.) Serve with duckling. Serves 2.

SUGARBUSH BOMBE

Combine 1 envelope (1 tablespoon) unflavored gelatin, 1 cup sugar, and 1 tablespoon cornstarch in a saucepan. Blend in 2 cups milk. Cook, stirring constantly, over medium heat till mixture thickens and boils. Remove from heat; stir small amount of hot mixture into 3 slightly beaten egg yolks, then return to hot mixture. Stirring constantly, bring to a boil; cook and stir 2 minutes longer. Remove from heat; stir in ¼ cup pure maple syrup. Cool till partially set. Fold in 1 cup ground hazelnuts and 3 stiffly beaten egg whites. Then fold in 1 cup whipping cream, whipped. Pour into a 1½ quart mold; chill till set, about 3 hours. Unmold; serve with maple syrup. Serves 8.

TRUITE FARCIE

6 mushrooms, thinly sliced
2 leeks, cut in julienne strips
1 medium carrot, cut in julienne strips
1 medium celery branch, cut in julienne strips
1 truffle, thinly sliced
¼ cup butter or margarine
¼ cup port
2 tablespoons cognac
2 tablespoons dry vermouth
6 trout, boned
Salt and pepper to taste
1 cup dry white wine
1 cup Court Bouillon
4 egg yolks
½ cup whipping cream
Salt and pepper to taste

Cook vegetables in ¼ cup butter for 2 to 3 minutes. Add port, cognac, and dry vermouth. Cook about 2 minutes longer or till liquid is reduced to a glaze. Season inside of trout with salt and pepper. Stuff with vegetable mixture. Poach fish in enough white wine to cover, about 1 cup, for 5 minutes or until fish flakes. Remove fish to hot platter; keep warm. To make sauce, combine Court Bouillon with egg yolks and cream. Beat over *hot, not boiling* water till thickened. Season with salt and pepper; pour over stuffed trout. Sprinkle with paprika and garnish with lemon wedges. Makes 6 servings.

COURT BOUILLON

¼ cup *each* chopped celery, chopped carrot, and chopped onion
1 small bay leaf
2 peppercorns
1 whole clove
1 teaspoon salt
1½ teaspoons snipped parsley
2 cups water
1 tablespoon white vinegar

Combine all ingredients. Bring to boiling; reduce heat and simmer, uncovered, till liquid is reduced to 1 cup. Strain before using.

Note: Try poaching fish in Court Bouillon for a wonderful herb flavor.

CHICKEN LIVERS WITH BEARNAISE SAUCE

¼ cup butter or margarine
1 tablespoon lemon juice
Dash salt
6 large fresh mushroom caps
2 tablespoons finely chopped onion
¼ cup dry sherry
6 pairs chicken livers (1 8-ounce package frozen)

• • •

1 tablespoon white vinegar
1 tablespoon water
1 tablespoon finely chopped green onion
½ teaspoon cracked black pepper
Dash crushed tarragon
Dash salt

• • •

2 egg yolks
2 tablespoons water
¼ cup butter or margarine, melted

• • •

Salt and pepper to taste
Paprika

Melt ¼ cup butter in a large skillet; stir in lemon juice and salt. Add fresh mushroom caps, tops down; simmer for 3 to 4 minutes. Remove mushrooms to a 10x6x1½-inch baking dish; keep warm. Cook chopped onions in the skillet until tender but not brown; stir in sherry. Add chicken livers; cover and cook over low heat till tender, about 5 to 7 minutes; keep warm.

Make a Bearnaise Sauce: Combine 1 tablespoon vinegar, 1 tablespoon water, chopped green onion, cracked black pepper, crushed tarragon, and dash salt in a small saucepan; simmer 2 to 3 miutes or until onions are tender. Remove from heat and cool. Beat egg yolks with 2 tablespoons water until thick and lemon colored. Very slowly add ¼ cup melted butter, beating constantly. Gently blend in cooled vinegar mixture. (Makes about 1½ cups sauce.)

To assemble, place a pair of chicken livers on each mushroom cap; sprinkle with salt, pepper, and paprika. Cover filled mushrooms with Bearnaise Sauce. Heat in a moderate oven (350°) for 8 to 10 minutes. Serve immediately. Makes 6 servings.

BARQUETTE OF TINY SHRIMP

1½ cups sifted all-purpose flour
½ teaspoon salt
½ cup shortening
4 to 5 tablespoons cold water

• • •

1 tablespoon salt
3 cups water
1 pound tiny shrimp in shell, or 2 4½-ounce cans shrimp
2 tablespoons finely chopped celery
1 tablespoon chopped shallots
½ teaspoon dill weed
½ cup catsup
2 tablespoons lemon juice
2 tablespoons mayonnaise
2 teaspoons prepared mustard
1 teaspoon prepared horseradish

Sift together flour and salt. Cut in shortening with pastry-blender or blending fork till pieces are size of small peas. Sprinkle 1 tablespoon of the water over part of flour-shortening mixture. Gently toss with fork; push to one side of bowl. Sprinkle next tablespoon water over dry part, mix lightly; push to moistened part at side. Repeat till all is moistened. Gather up with fingers; form into a ball.

On lightly floured surface, roll dough to 14x15-inch rectangle. Top with same size aluminum foil; mark in 3x2-inch rectangles. Cut small rectangles with scissors, cutting through pastry and foil at the same time. Turn each rectangle pastry side up; prick well with fork. Moisten 2-inch ends of pastry; pinch together (along with foil) to form "boats," (foil will help keep the shape while baking). Place "boats" on baking sheet; spread sides to keep upright. Bake in hot oven (425°) for about 10 minutes or until lightly browned. Cool. Remove foil.

Add the salt to the water; bring to boiling. Add shrimp; cover and heat to boiling. Reduce heat and simmer gently till shrimp turn pink, about 5 minutes. Drain. Peel and devein shrimp; chop fine. Combine with remaining ingredients; mix well. Chill. Fill pastry boats with shrimp; garnish with chopped black olives and sieved egg yolk. Serve as appetizer. Makes about 3 dozen.

Fancy kabobs on rice! Lamb Shish Kabob (left), Sea-food Kabobs (right top), and Beef Kabobs (front) served with hot Kous Koush for "old world" touch.

While dining high above the ground in this handsome blue and gold room, guests enjoy a dramatic view of the World's Fair and Manhattan skyline.

UNISPHERE®

NEW YORK'S WORLD FAIR

Top of the Fair

This glass-enclosed restaurant is part of the exciting 1964-65 World's Fair in New York City. Suspended high above the fairgrounds, it is on the upper floor of the Port Authority Heliport and Exhibit Building, and helicopters actually take off and land on the roof! The giant picture windows in the restaurant afford a panoramic view of the Fair and New York City's skyline, and the dining room is built on three levels to insure everyone of good visibility. The interior has been strikingly decorated by Arturo Pini De San Miniato in the official blue and gold colors of the Fair. Executive Chef Charles Peponakis shares his recipes for shish kabobs (left), including the tangy marinade, and his recipe for deliciously rich and creamy Chocolate Creme which he serves three ways—as a pie, a sherbet dessert, and a spectacular torte, (all pictured on the next page).

LAMB SHISH KABOBS

3 to 3½ pounds boneless lamb, cut in 2-inch cubes
Top of the Fair Marinade
5 medium onions
4 medium green peppers
3 medium tomatoes, quartered

Add lamb cubes to marinade; stir to coat. Let stand in refrigerator for 2 days, turning meat several times. Peel and quarter onions; make each quarter into a "cup" by removing a few center leaves. Cut the four sides off the green peppers. From each side carve an oval. (This prevents burned corners on the finished kabobs.) On 4 skewers (12 inches long) string pieces of onion, lamb, green pepper, and tomato (put piece of onion on skewer first to season skewer). Brush kabobs with the marinade. Broil 4 to 5 inches from heat for 15 minutes. Turn and brush with the marinade. Broil 10 minutes longer. Serves 4. Serve on rice, if desired.

SEA-FOOD KABOBS

4 king crab legs (about
3½ pounds, unshelled)
5 medium onions
4 medium green peppers
4 medium tomatoes, quartered
¼ cup lemon juice
¼ cup butter or margarine, melted

Remove crab meat from cracked shells; cut in 2-inch pieces. Prepare onion cups and green pepper ovals as in Lamb Shish Kabob. On 4 skewers (about 12 inches long), string pieces of onion, crab, tomato, and green pepper. Mix lemon juice and butter; brush over kabobs. Broil 3 inches from heat for 7 minutes. Turn; brush with lemon juice and butter mixture; broil 7 minutes longer. To serve, pass drawn butter and lemon wedges. Makes 4 servings.

TOP OF THE FAIR MARINADE

Combine ½ cup salad or peanut oil, ¼ cup lemon juice, 1 teaspoon salt, 1 teaspoon crushed oregano, ½ teaspoon pepper, and 1 clove garlic, minced. Use to marinate lamb or beef—enough for 3 to 3½ pounds.

BEEF KABOBS

Refrigerate 2 pounds beef tenderloin or sirloin tip, in 2-inch pieces, in Top of the Fair Marinade for 1 day, turning several times. Prepare onion cups, green pepper ovals, quartered tomatoes as in Lamb Shish Kabobs. On 4 skewers (12 inches long) string pieces of onion, beef, green pepper, and tomato; brush with marinade. Broil 4 to 5 inches from heat 10 minutes. Turn; brush with marinade. Broil 10 minutes longer. Serve with hot Kous Koush. Serves 4.

KOUS KOUSH

1⅓ cups cracked (bulgur) wheat
2⅔ cups chicken broth
½ teaspoon salt
Dash pepper
¼ cup butter or margarine

Toast cracked wheat in skillet, stirring often, (15 minutes). Add remaining ingredients; bring to full boil. Pour into 1½-quart casserole. Cover; bake at 350° for 15 minutes. Uncover; stir. Bake uncovered 15 minutes more. Fluff with fork; top with tomato wedges and snipped parsley. Serves 8.

Chocolate Creme goes into these 3 fancy desserts—Top of the Fair Torte, Chocolate Creme Dessert, and Chef Charles Pie. Each is trimmed with whipped cream and chocolate curls.

CHOCOLATE CREME

⅓ cup sugar
2 tablespoons cornstarch
1 envelope (1 tablespoon) unflavored gelatin
¼ teaspoon salt

• • •

2 cups milk
2 1-ounce squares unsweetened chocolate
3 slightly beaten egg yolks

• • •

3 unbeaten egg whites
1 teaspoon vanilla
⅓ cup sugar

Thoroughly mix ⅓ cup sugar, cornstarch, gelatin, and salt in a saucepan. Blend in milk; add chocolate. Cook over medium heat, stirring constantly, till mixture thickens and comes to a boil. Remove from heat. Stir small amount hot mixture into yolks, blend into hot mixture. Bring to boil; cook and stir 1 minute. Cool 15 minutes.

Beat the egg whites and vanilla till soft peaks form. Slowly add ⅓ cup sugar; beat until stiff peaks form. Fold in chocolate mixture gradually, blending well. Makes 4½ cups filling; enough for Top of the Fair Torte, or Chef Charles Pie, or 8 sherbets of Chocolate Creme Dessert.

CHOCOLATE CREME DESSERT

1 recipe Chocolate Creme

• • •

½ cup whipping cream
1 teaspoon sugar
Chocolate Curls
Maraschino cherries

Prepare Chocolate Creme filling; chill till it mounds slightly when spooned. Pile the filling into 8 sherbet glasses.

Whip cream with sugar. Pipe whipped cream through a rosette pastry tube to form rosettes over top of dessert on each sherbet. Garnish with Chocolate Curls (for how-to, see recipe for Chef Charles Pie). Top each serving with a maraschino cherry. Chill dessert thoroughly. Makes 8 servings.

TOP OF THE FAIR TORTE

1 recipe Chocolate Creme
1 9-inch layer sponge cake
2 cups whipping cream
2 tablespoons granulated sugar

• • •

½ cup sliced almonds, toasted
Chocolate Curls
Confectioners' sugar

Prepare Chocolate Creme filling; chill till it mounds slightly when spooned. Split cake layer to make 2 thin layers. Carefully spoon chilled mixture over bottom layer; spread to smooth. Chill 30 minutes. Top with second cake layer.

Whip cream with granulated sugar. Frost top and sides of cake with 2½ *cups of the* whipped cream. Pipe remaining whipped cream through a rosette pastry tube to form a lattice top. Pipe around edge of cake, looping whipped cream over ends of lattice. Garnish sides of torte with almonds. Top cake with Chocolate Curls (for how-to see Chef Charles Pie). Sift confectioners' sugar over. Chill at least 2 hours to set filling. Makes 10 to 12 servings.

CHEF CHARLES PIE

1 recipe Chocolate Creme
1 9-inch baked pastry shell
1 cup whipping cream
1 tablespoon granulated sugar

• • •

Chocolate Curls
Confectioners' sugar

Prepare Chocolate Creme filling; chill till it mounds slightly when spooned. Pile into cooled pastry shell; chill until firm.

Whip cream with sugar. Frost pie with whipped cream, reserving some to pipe through a rosette pastry tube to form rosettes around edge of the pie. Trim with Chocolate Curls. Dust with confectioners' sugar. Chill till serving time.

Chocolate Curls: Have one 4-ounce package sweet cooking chocolate *at room temperature.* Using potato peeler, carefully shave off thin slices of the chocolate—it will curl as you cut.

SAUERBRATEN

3 to 3½ pounds beef round or rump, cut thick
1 teaspoon salt
½ teaspoon pepper
4 bay leaves
½ teaspoon peppercorns
8 whole cloves
2 medium onions, sliced
1 small carrot, minced
1 stalk celery (1 piece), chopped
1½ cups red wine vinegar
2½ cups water
¼ cup butter

• • •

Gingersnap Gravy

Thoroughly rub meat with the salt and pepper. Place meat in deep earthenware crock or ovenware glass bowl with all the spices and vegetables. Heat the vinegar and water to boiling and pour *hot* over the meat. Let cool. Cover bowl well and refrigerate. Let marinate at least 48 hours, turning the meat twice a day.

When ready to cook, remove meat from marinade and dry with paper towels. Melt butter in Dutch oven or kettle and brown the meat all over. Strain the marinade and pour over meat. Then put on a tight-fitting cover. Let simmer slowly 2½ to 3 hours or until fork tender. Remove meat to warmed serving platter, slice, and keep warm while making Gingersnap Gravy. Serves 6.

GINGERSNAP GRAVY

2 tablespoons sugar
1½ cups hot marinade
½ cup water
⅔ cup gingersnap crumbs (takes about 8 gingersnaps)
Salt

For 2 cups gravy, melt the sugar in a skillet, stirring all the while until a nice golden brown. Gradually stir in hot marinade and water. Add gingersnap crumbs; cook, stirring constantly, until mixture thickens. (If you like, stir in ½ cup dairy sour cream.) Salt gravy to taste. Ladle some over Sauerbraten and pass remainder in a bowl.

NEW YORK CITY

Lüchow's

A haven of Gemütlichkeit (comfortable geniality) of years gone by, Lüchow's is located on East 14th Street in busy New York. Once the center of New York's night life, East 14th is now a noisy street of bargain shops, worn buildings, and swarms of hurried, hustling shoppers. In these rakish surroundings, Lüchow's retains its old world traditions and romance through 81 years of hospitality and the best in food and service.

Founded in 1882 by jolly, rotund Herr August Lüchow, it is now owned by Swedish-born Jan Mitchell. Mr. Mitchell is a European-trained restaurateur whose pledge is to keep Lüchow's and the glories of its German kitchen unchanged. He has preserved the robust character and traditions, brought back original German delicacies to the menu and revived the festivals, such as Christmas, Venison, Goose and Wine. And the Viennese orchestra still entertains diners with Herbert music and Strauss waltzes.

Amidst the warmth and splendor of dark mahogany paneling, enormous mirrors, prized oil paintings, gaslight chandeliers, and great antique steins, have dined celebrities and gourmets from all parts of the world. Truly it is, as the menu states, "the gourmet's rendezvous."

It was William Steinway of piano fame, with his $1,500 loan, who set August Lüchow up in business and who ate there daily. Today, the fifth-generation Steinway frequently dines here. At left, in the Steinway Room, Fred Hacker, for 45 years a Lüchow waiter, is carving a famous dish—Sauerbraten (a favorite of Diamond Jim Brady when he was a steady patron). With it are Kartoffel Klösse and Kartoffel Pfannkuchen (Potato Dumpling and Potato Pancakes).

KARTOFFEL KLÖSSE
(*Potato Dumpling*)

6 medium potatoes, pared (2 pounds)
2 slightly beaten eggs
¾ cup all-purpose flour
½ cup farina
⅛ teaspoon nutmeg
⅛ teaspoon cinnamon
½ teaspoon sugar
1 teaspoon salt

Boil potatoes and put through a ricer (about 4½ cups); let cool. Add remaining ingredients in order; beat well. Roll mixture into balls (golf ball size). Drop balls into plenty of boiling salted water to cover (1 teaspoon salt to 1 quart water).* Let simmer 20 minutes. Lift out; serve hot, sprinkled with parsley. (If desired, spread tops of hot dumplings with crumb mixture: Brown 2 tablespoons minced onion and 1 cup fine dry bread crumbs in ¼ cup butter.) Serves 6.

*It's a good idea first to shape and test one dumpling in the boiling water. If it falls apart, beat a little more flour into remaining dumpling mixture.

Elegant desserts climax Lüchow meals. In center (and sliced at left) is Cherry Torte, Black Forest Style. Also on platter are Lüchow's apple strudel, and, to the rear, incredibly light Almond Horns.

KARTOFFEL PFANNKUCHEN
(*Potato Pancakes*)

Pare 6 medium potatoes; cover with cold water; drain. Grate at once; drain off water that collects. Add 1 small onion, grated, 2 tablespoons flour, 4 strips bacon which have been crisply cooked and crumbled, 2 beaten eggs, 1½ teaspoons salt, pinch *each* of pepper and grated nutmeg, and 2 tablespoons chopped parsley; blend well. Heat enough butter in a skillet to be ¼ inch deep. Just before it turns brown, drop in ⅓ cup batter for each pancake; flatten. Brown one side; turn and brown other side. Remove to paper towels; keep warm. Makes 12.

CHERRY TORTE, BLACK FOREST STYLE

1 1-pound can pitted dark sweet cherries
⅓ cup kirsch
1½ tablespoons cornstarch
1 cup moderately soft butter (½ pound)
4½ cups sifted confectioners' sugar
3 egg yolks
2 8-inch spongecake layers, 1 inch thick
Chocolate shot
1 1-ounce square semisweet chocolate, finely shaved (⅓ cup)

For filling: drain, (reserving ¾ cup syrup), and halve cherries; pour kirsch over; let stand 2 hours. In saucepan, gradually blend reserved syrup into cornstarch; add cherries. Heat and stir quickly till mixture thickens and boils; cook and stir 1 minute. Cool. Chill. For butter-cream, beat butter and sugar till smooth; beat in yolks till light and fluffy. Place 1 layer spongecake on plate. Using 1 cup butter-cream, make ½-inch border (1¼ inches high) around top of cake. Using ½ cup butter-cream, make circle in center of cake, 2½ inches in diameter (1¼ inches high). Spread chilled filling between border and center of butter-cream. Top with second cake layer; press lightly. Cover torte with remaining butter-cream. Sprinkle sides with chocolate shot, and the top with shaved chocolate; trim with maraschino cherries. Chill. Let stand at room temperature 20 minutes before serving. Serves 6 to 8.

LÜCHOW'S ALMOND HORNS

¼ pound soft butter (½ cup or 1 stick)
½ cup sugar
5 slightly beaten eggs

• • •

2 packages active dry yeast
⅓ cup *warm* water
⅔ cup milk, scalded
5½ to 6 cups sifted all-purpose flour

• • •

¼ pound butter (½ cup or 1 stick), firm, but not brittle-cold
Almond Filling:
½ pound (1 cup) almond paste
⅔ cup sugar
1 egg
Sliced almonds

Thoroughly mix the soft butter, sugar, and eggs. Soften yeast in the water. Cool milk to lukewarm, then stir into egg mixture along with softened yeast. Last, add enough flour to make soft dough, mixing well. Refrigerate dough for 3 hours to chill.

On lightly floured surface, roll dough to a 14-inch square, about ½ inch thick. Now roll in remaining butter this way; Dot the butter over *half* the dough, then fold other half of dough over butter-dotted area; seal edges. Now roll the dough to a 20x12-inch rectangle, ¼ inch thick. Fold dough in thirds; seal edges and repeat this step 3 more times, chilling dough after each rolling if it softens. Put the dough back in refrigerator until next day (or until well chilled).

Next day, divide dough in fourths. On lightly floured surface, roll each piece to a 15-inch circle, about ⅛ inch thick. Cut each circle in 6 wedges like a pie. Along the side opposite the point, put about 1 tablespoon Almond Filling; roll up, going toward point. Place point down on greased baking sheet. Cover and let rise in warm place until almost double, about 30 to 45 minutes. Just before placing in oven, brush tops of horns with mixture of 1 slightly beaten egg yolk mixed with 1 tablespoon water. Sprinkle with almonds. Bake in moderate oven (350°) for about 20 to 25 minutes or till done. Serve warm. Makes 2 dozen.

Almond Filling: Thoroughly mix the almond paste, ⅔ cup sugar, and egg.

HUHN IM TOPF
(*Chicken in Casserole*)

1 3-pound whole ready-to-cook broiler-fryer chicken
4 carrots, cut on the bias in 1½-inch lengths
2 small turnips, halved
1 cup cut green beans (raw)
2 medium leeks or green onions, sliced
2 stalks (2 pieces) celery, sliced
1 clove garlic studded with 1 whole clove (spice)
1 bay leaf
1 cup green peas (raw)
4 ounces medium noodles
Marrow Dumplings
1 tablespoon chopped parsley

Place chicken and giblets in a pot. Half cover with cold water; bring to boiling; skim. Salt cooking water lightly; add carrots, turnips, beans, leeks, celery, garlic, and bay leaf. Cover and simmer slowly 30 minutes, turning chicken once. Add peas and noodles; cook 10 minutes more or till chicken is nearly tender. Add Marrow Dumplings to broth; let simmer 10 to 12 minutes or till everything is done. Transfer chicken, vegetables, noodles, and dumplings to casserole. Add parsley and some pepper to the broth (first discard bay leaf and garlic with clove); pour over chicken, trim with parsley. Serve boiling hot. Makes 6 servings.

MARROW DUMPLINGS

1½ tablespoons fresh marrow (from a 3-inch length of beef bone), strained through a fine sieve
1 tablespoon soft butter
1 whole egg and 1 yolk of egg beaten together with pinch of grated nutmeg
⅔ cup cracker or matzoth crumbs
Pinch of baking powder
Salt and pepper to taste
1 tablespoon chopped parsley

Combine ingredients; mix till smooth. (Add more cracker crumbs if needed to hold mixture together.) Form small marble-size balls; cook as directed in *Huhn im Topf*. Makes about 2 dozen dumplings.

NEW YORK CITY

Four Seasons

The Four Seasons opened in the summer of 1959 on the lobby floor of the Seagram Building. The owners, Restaurant Associates, Inc., insisted that it be harmonious with the spectacular architectural style of the building itself. The result is a showcase that rivals any of New York's many fine restaurants.

The cuisine of the Four Seasons lives up to the excitement of its architectural setting. Many of the dishes presented on the menu are refreshingly different; some are utterly original. As you could guess, there are four changes of menu every year. The man behind the extraordinary food is Albert Stockli, Chef Director of the Associates. Prices are on the side of being high, nevertheless, the restaurant is flourishing and has been a success from the first day. This seems to indicate that there are many who bask in its classic grandeur, who love its food and wines, and are more than pleased to pay for the privilege of enjoying them.

SAUTEED CALF'S LIVER WITH AVOCADO

1½ pounds calf's liver
¼ cup butter
2 medium avocados
¼ cup butter
½ cup chicken broth
⅓ cup white wine
¼ cup lemon juice
1 tablespoon snipped chives
1 teaspoon snipped parsley

Slice liver in 12 thin slices. In a skillet quickly brown liver on both sides in 2 *tablespoons* butter. Remove to a platter and keep warm. Cut each avocado in 9 thin whole slices. In skillet cook avocado slices in 2 *tablespoons* butter, about 1 minute on each side. Remove to the platter with the cooked liver and keep warm.

In same skillet, brown ¼ cup butter. Add chicken broth, wine, lemon juice, chives, and parsley; bring to a boil. Pour mixture over liver and avocado slices. Makes 6 servings.

The Krebs
1899

SKANEATELES

The Krebs

The Krebs lives up to its reputation of being one of the most widely-discussed places to eat we have found. Mr. and Mrs. Frederic W. Perkins, long familiar with gourmet eating and gourmet cooking, serve a most generous table d'hote dinner which they vary with the bounty of the changing seasons. The 39 West Genesee Street restaurant was opened in 1899 by Mr. and Mrs. Fred R. Krebs. Through the years it has become a haven attracting travelers from coast to coast, luring many to change their course in order to enjoy huge home-cooked dinners of a kind now almost vanished from our eating experience.

The generosity of the servings at The Krebs is reason enough to forget all concern for weight-watching and calorie-counting. No menu delays your decision as to what to order, for the one meal that's offered is sure to please. Serving dishes filled with excellently prepared food are presented with a flourish for you to serve yourself. Only your appetite guides the size of your portion at The Krebs. From the first Sunday in May to the last Sunday in October, dinner is served each day of the week except Friday.

CREAM OF PEANUT SOUP

¼ cup finely chopped onion
1½ cups chicken broth
1 cup creamy peanut butter, softened
¼ cup finely chopped salted peanuts
4 cups light cream
½ teaspoon salt
Dash white pepper

Cook onions in broth for 7 to 8 minutes or till tender. *Slowly* add broth with onions to the softened peanut butter, stirring constantly. Return mixture to saucepan; add peanuts. Gradually add cream, stirring constantly; heat thoroughly (*do not boil*). Add salt and pepper. Top each serving with a dollop of whipped cream and sprinkle with paprika. Makes 8 to 12 servings.

WATER GATE
INN

WASHINGTON, D.C.

Water Gate Inn

Mention popovers in the Washington area and you can only be talking about one place: Marjory Hendricks' Water Gate Inn located on the Potomac at F Street, N. W. The Inn's Pennsylvania Dutch interior is a masterpiece of Early American decoration. Especially interesting is its striking collection of century-old hobby-horses, which led to the use of the rocking horse as their symbol.

The little wooden man on the horse opposite, watches over a tasty appetizer of Herbed Mushrooms. The Hot Popovers are the specialty of the house. Just taste one and you'll know why. Other Pennsylvania Dutch dishes are Mennonite Chicken Baked in Sour Cream, shown in individual frying pans, Chicken Barbara, a recipe originated by Mrs. Hendricks, and Duck Mit Sauerkraut Fritztown, truly a Dutch dish which is popular and frequently served.

MENNONITE CHICKEN BAKED IN SOUR CREAM

¼ cup butter or margarine
¼ cup all-purpose flour
1 teaspoon salt
Dash pepper
1 2-pound ready-to-cook broiler-fryer chicken, split in half
Paprika
3 tablespoons water
1 tablespoon all-purpose flour
¼ teaspoon salt
Dash *each* pepper and paprika
½ cup dairy sour cream

Place butter in shallow baking pan or oven-going skillet; heat to melt butter. Combine ¼ cup flour, salt and dash pepper; roll chicken in mixture till coated. Dip coated chicken in melted butter and arrange skin side up in the baking pan. Sprinkle with paprika. Bake in slow oven (325°) for 1¼ hours or till chicken is tender and nicely browned. Remove chicken from pan; keep warm.

Add water to pan drippings; mix well. Blend in 1 tablespoon flour, ¼ teaspoon salt, dash *each* pepper and paprika, and ½ cup sour cream. Bring to a boil, stirring constantly. Remove from heat and serve over chicken. Makes 2 servings.

HERBED MUSHROOMS

½ teaspoon dill weed
1 clove garlic, halved
⅓ cup *each* red wine vinegar and water
2 tablespoons butter or margarine, melted
1 pint mushroom caps
Nutmeg

Combine first 4 ingredients and set aside. Meanwhile, butter tops of mushrooms; sprinkle lightly with nutmeg and broil 5 minutes. Place mushrooms in a jar and pour vinegar mixture over; refrigerate. Chill mushrooms in mixture at least 3 hours.

MARJORY HENDRICKS' POPOVERS

1 cup all-purpose flour
1 teaspoon salt
3 eggs
1 cup milk
2 tablespoons whipping cream

Stir flour and salt together; make well in center and add eggs, milk, and cream. Beat for 3 minutes. Cover batter; chill thoroughly, about 2 hours. Heat iron popover pan thoroughly in a very hot oven (450°); grease quickly with oil. Fill cups almost to brim; return to hot oven. Bake for 22 minutes; reduce temperature to 375° and bake 13 minutes longer. Loosen popovers from pan and serve immediately. Makes 8.

DUCK MIT SAUERKRAUT FRITZTOWN

1 3- to 3½-pound duckling
1 14-ounce can (2 cups) sauerkraut
1 medium onion, sliced
2 tablespoons sugar
Dash pepper

Clean duck for roasting. Rub inside with salt; stuff with 2 cups sauerkraut. Prick skin and truss. Place breast up on rack in shallow baking pan. Arrange onion slices atop duck. Cover with foil and bake at 375° for 1½ hours. Uncover, remove onion slices. Drain off excess fat. Sprinkle duck with sugar and pepper. Return to oven; roast till brown, about 30 minutes. Makes 3 to 4 servings.

CHICKEN BARBARA

3 large chicken breasts
1 teaspoon salt
¼ teaspoon pepper
1 teaspoon rosemary
1 branch celery, tops and leaves
1 large onion, sliced (about 1½ cups)
1 cup water
1 clove garlic, halved

. . .

1 cup sifted all-purpose flour
1½ teaspoons baking powder
¼ teaspoon salt
1 beaten egg yolk
⅔ cup milk
¼ cup salad oil
1 stiffly beaten egg white

. . .

¾ cup reserved chicken stock
3 tablespoons all-purpose flour
½ teaspoon salt
Dash pepper
¾ cup light cream
1 tablespoon lemon juice
2 drops yellow food coloring

Place chicken breasts in 2 quart casserole. Sprinkle with 1 teaspoon salt, ¼ teaspoon pepper, and rosemary; add celery, onion, and water. Cover and bake in moderate oven (375°) till tender, about 1 hour. Reserve stock; cool chicken. Remove skin and bones; cut each breast in half and rub well with a freshly cut clove of garlic. Set aside while preparing batter and cream sauce.

Batter: Sift together 1 cup flour, baking powder, and ¼ teaspoon salt. Combine beaten egg yolk, milk, and oil; stir into dry ingredients. Fold in stiffly beaten egg white, leaving a few fluffs—don't overmix. Dip halved chicken breasts in batter. Fry in deep hot fat (375°) until nicely browned, about 3 minutes. Serve hot with Cream Sauce.

Cream Sauce: Heat ¾ cup of the reserved chicken stock in a saucepan over low heat. Blend in 3 tablespoons flour, ½ teaspoon salt and dash pepper. Add light cream; stir and cook quickly till mixture thickens slightly and bubbles. Stir in lemon juice and 2 drops yellow food coloring. Serve chicken atop Cream Sauce. Makes 6 servings.

Hogate's

WASHINGTON, D. C.

Hogate's

Hogate's Sea Food Restaurant overlooks the banks of the Potomac but the map says it's on the corner of 9th Street and Maine Avenue Southwest, Washington, D.C. Nautical in its decor, it's a favorite gathering place for people who search for good food. Guests can see their dinner being prepared through the glass windows which give them full view of the kitchen. As originators of the Mariner's Platter, a sampler plate of flounder, deviled crab, deviled clams, fried oysters, scallops, and shrimp salad, they are now world famous for this specialty. Hogate's is also known for Clam Chowder, the kind made with fresh clams!

HOGATE'S CLAM CHOWDER

2 dozen medium hard-shell clams
6 cups hot water
2 ounces (¾ cup) salt pork, diced
2 cups (about 3 medium) diced potatoes
1 cup chopped onion
1 teaspoon thyme
1 1-pound can (2 cups) tomatoes
2 tablespoons all-purpose flour
¼ cup cold water

Thoroughly wash clams in shell. Cover with salt water (⅓ cup salt to 1 gallon cold water); let stand 15 minutes. Rinse with unsalted water; repeat 2 more times. Place clams on rack in kettle and cover with 6 cups hot water. Cover kettle tightly and steam just till shells open (about 10 minutes). Remove clams reserving 4 cups cooking liquor. Shuck clams and dice.

Brown salt pork in large sauce pan. Add 2 cups of the liquor, potatoes, onion, and thyme. Cook till potatoes are almost done, about 20 minutes. Add tomatoes and remaining 2 cups of liquor. Bring to a boil.

Blend 2 tablespoons flour with ¼ cup cold water to make a smooth paste. Stir into chowder; cook and stir till mixture comes to a boil. Add clams; heat through. Serves 8.

BOUILLABAISSE SOUP

- ½ pound green shrimp
- ½ pound codfish
- ½ pound scallops
- 6 oysters
- 1 teaspoon salt
- 2 tablespoons minced onion
- 1 clove garlic, minced
- 2 tablespoons minced celery
- 2 tablespoons minced green pepper
- ½ cup butter or margarine
- ½ cup all-purpose flour
- 1 cup cooked lobster (about 1½ pounds whole, or 1 medium-sized lobster tail)

Shell and clean shrimp, saving shells. Tie codfish in cheesecloth; place codfish, scallops, shrimp, and oysters in 2 quarts salted water; bring to boil. Reduce heat, simmer 5 minutes; drain, reserving stock. Place shrimp shells in reserved stock and cook till liquid is reduced to 4 cups. Strain stock through a cheesecloth. Cook onion, garlic, celery, and green pepper in butter till tender. Add flour, then stir in 2 cups stock; cook and stir till thickened.

Dice codfish, scallops, shrimp, and lobster; add to thickened soup with oysters; heat through. (Store remaining fish stock for future use.) Makes 4 to 6 servings.

OLD ORIGINAL
BOOKBINDER'S

PHILADELPHIA

Old Original Bookbinder's

Revered Philadelphia landmark, renowned for sea food for almost 100 years (since 1865), the Old Original Bookbinder's is located near the water front at 125 Walnut Street. Evidence of their high standards of cuisine and service is this paragraph printed on the back of their menus, "Today at the restaurant, we do our utmost to carry on a 99-year tradition of fine food, that has made Old Original Bookbinder's famous throughout the world. We have only one criterion in purchasing for our kitchens: 'Is it the very finest quality the market offers? Does it meet Old Original Bookbinder's standards?' We hope we please you and we appreciate your patronage most sincerely."

John Taxin, host and president of Old Original Bookbinder's, permits in his restaurant only live, kicking lobsters which are flown fresh from Nova Scotia waters to Bookbinder's own lobster tanks. The clams and oysters Mr. Taxin serves at the Bookbinder's are raised under supervision and are "fresh as the morning paper—and washed within an inch of their lives!"

In the picture on the opposite page, you see on Mr. Taxin's left, a large bowl of Bookbinder's famous Snapper Soup which is delicately laced with sherry. On the platter in the foreground are piping-hot Broiled Scallops garnished with parsley sprigs and lemon wedges and served with a side dish of tangy Tartare Sauce. To top off the meal, he suggests a generous slice of chocolate-almond cake. The recipe for Bouillabaisse Soup is also given—a delicious combination of shrimp, codfish, scallops, oysters, and lobster in one hearty dish.

BOOKBINDER'S SNAPPER SOUP

1½ pounds veal knuckle, in 2-inch pieces
¼ cup butter
1 cup chopped onion
1 branch celery, chopped
1 small carrot, diced
1 teaspoon salt
1 whole clove
1 small bay leaf
¼ teaspoon *each* pepper and thyme
¼ cup flour
3 cans condensed beef broth
1 cup canned tomatoes
1 pound frozen snapper turtle meat, cut in small pieces
½ cup dry sherry
Dash bottled hot pepper sauce
1 slice lemon

Place first 10 ingredients in shallow roasting pan. Bake at 400° for 30 minutes. Push bones to one side; blend in flour; bake at 350° for 30 minutes longer. Transfer to kettle; add broth and tomatoes; cover, simmer 1½ hours. Meanwhile, simmer turtle meat, covered, in ¾ cup water 1 to 1½ hours, or till tender; add last 3 ingredients; cover, simmer 10 minutes. Strain veal soup; skim off fat. Combine veal and turtle soups; heat; season with salt and pepper. Serves 6.

BROILED SCALLOPS

1 pound scallops

• • •

Salt to taste
Pepper to taste
Dash paprika
Butter

Place 1 pound scallops in shallow pan or pie plate. Sprinkle with salt, pepper, and paprika, then dot with butter.

Broil 3 inches from heat for 6 to 9 minutes or until scallops are very delicately browned, spooning pan drippings over scallops several times. To serve, garnish with lemon wedges and sprigs of parsley; pass Tartare Sauce. Makes 2 to 3 servings.

TARTARE SAUCE

1 cup mayonnaise
2 tablespoons minced parsley
1 tablespoon minced onion
1 tablespoon chopped stuffed green olives
2 tablespoons well drained green pickle relish

Combine all ingredients in a mixing bowl. Mix well. Refrigerate sauce 3 hours before serving. Serve with Broiled Scallops.

Bookbinder's Snapper Soup is a delightful combination of veal and turtle delicately laced with sherry. Pass chopped hard-cooked egg to add to soup.

Spoon the pan drippings over Broiled Scallops several times while cooking. To serve, garnish with lemon wedges and parsley; pass tangy Tartare Sauce.

Le Mont

PITTSBURGH

Le Mont

The spirit of this dynamic city glows through its night lights. From the top of Mt. Washington, Le Mont looks over Pittsburgh's Golden Triangle formed by the meeting of the Allegheny and Monongahela Rivers. Le Mont reflects the boldness of the city—from deep red carpeting to immense glass walls. The cuisine, influenced by French cookery, is served with flourish and formality. Elegance is the feeling with which guests depart from the mountain.

BAKED BELGIUM ENDIVE ROLLED IN HAM "LeMont"

4 heads Belgian endive, 2- to 4-ounces each
¼ cup water
2 tablespoons lemon juice
½ teaspoon salt
Dash pepper
2 5-ounce packages Danish Imported Ham

• • •

2 tablespoons butter or margarine
2 tablespoons all-purpose flour
½ cup milk
½ cup chicken broth
1 cup shredded sharp process cheese

• • •

4 teaspoons grated Parmesan cheese

Wash endive and trim bottoms. In small saucepan, combine water, lemon juice, salt, and pepper. Add the endive. Cover and simmer for 10 minutes. Drain thoroughly. Roll each head in 2 ham slices, (put together to form a double thickness). Place each roll in a 4x4-inch individual casserole.

Melt butter in saucepan over low heat; blend in flour. Add milk and chicken broth all at once. Cook, stirring constantly, over low heat until mixture thickens and boils. Remove from heat; add shredded cheese and stir till cheese melts.

Top each roll with ⅓ cup of the cheese sauce. Sprinkle each with 1 teaspoon Parmesan. Bake in moderate oven (350°) for 15 minutes or till heated through. Serves 4.

BALTIMORE

Chesapeake

The appearance of a big mesh steamer filled with gaping soft-shelled clams may present an unappetizing sight to many diners. Not so to the clam lover! A huge kettle of steamed clams such as those pictured at left, accompanied by hot melted butter and the clam broth is invitation enough to "don the bib."

The Chesapeake Restaurant in Baltimore has served many a bib with many a kettle of clams. Then even through clam squirting and dripping butter, guests may enjoy this delicacy in safety. While the availability of clams, shrimp, scallops, oysters, crab, flounder, shad, and roe makes for a good beginning to excellent dishes, the Chesapeake adds experience and imagination to each creation. Even New Englanders used to the fruits of the sea are impressed.

In keeping with the cuisine, Chesapeake displays mural-sized photos of marine scenery. Deep seated comfort in red leather upholstering, subtly dim ship lamps, and mounted anchors are touches that bring the romance of the sea to the diner.

STEAMED CLAMS

2 dozen Chesapeake Bay soft shell clams, in shell
1 cup salt
3 gallons cold water
1 cup hot water

• • •

Melted butter or margarine
Lemon wedges

Scrub clams in cold water. To remove sand from clams, place in a solution of ⅓ *cup* salt to *1 gallon* cold water; let stand for 15 to 20 minutes. Sand will settle to bottom of container. Repeat 2 more times. Place clams on rack in kettle with 1 cup hot water; cover tightly and steam just till shells open, about 5 to 10 minutes. Drain off broth and save. Serve in shell with melted butter, reserved clam broth, and lemon. Serves 4 to 6.

LOCKE-OBER CAFE

WINTER PLACE

BOSTON

Locke-Ober Café

Since 1875 the Locke-Ober of Boston has been serving the best to the best. Beautiful antique covered servers (in the background at left) are used at the restaurant and are highly prized by today's patrons, according to President Charles Little. In the picture, Chef Martin Manzonetta is putting the final touches on a long-time favorite, Baked Lobster Savannah. The salad is Bibb lettuce drizzled with an excellent French Dressing. For sophisticated dessert, lemon sherbet is laced with green creme de menthe and served in stemmed glasses.

BAKED LOBSTER SAVANNAH

2 2-pound lobsters
½ cup sliced fresh mushrooms
¼ cup diced green pepper
3 tablespoons butter
2 tablespoons all-purpose flour
1 cup milk
¼ cup sherry
1 teaspoon paprika
2 tablespoons diced pimiento
Grated cheese
Fresh bread crumbs

Plunge lobsters in boiling salted water; cover and boil 25 minutes. Remove and let cool. Cut off claws and legs so only body remains. Hold lobster with its top side up; using kitchen shears, cut an oval opening in top of shell, from base of head to tail. Remove all meat from body and claws; cube. Cook mushrooms and green pepper in butter till tender. Blend in flour; add milk; cook and stir till mixture thickens and boils. Add sherry, paprika, and salt to taste; cook 5 minutes. Add lobster and pimiento. Pile filling in lobster shells; top with cheese and crumbs. Bake at 375° 15 minutes. Serves 2.

LOCKE-OBER FRENCH DRESSING

½ teaspoon *each* salt and dry mustard
¼ teaspoon white pepper
¼ teaspoon paprika
1 tablespoon lemon juice
⅓ cup cider vinegar
1 small clove garlic, crushed
1 cup salad oil

Combine all ingredients except oil; mix well, then add oil. Shake before use.

WILLIAMSBURG

Colonial Williamsburg

Charming is the word for the famous Williamsburg Inn, the Lodge, and the taverns in Williamsburg, Virginia. Here your family can bask in the warmth of Southern hospitality and step backward into the past and a gracious way of living. History's cast aside to give you the comfort of air conditioning. And the favorite foods of old Virginia are prepared in the most up-to-date kitchens.

Of all the holidays, Christmas comes closest to the spirit of eighteenth century Williamsburg. There's a fortnight of traditional holiday festivities during Christmas and New Year's annually. A colorful program includes yule log ceremonies, street caroling, candlelight concerts, dancing, musicals, fireworks, and wassailing. Hints of the holiday specialties of King's Arms Tavern are pictured opposite. Individual little Chicken Pyes, shown amidst the holly, Creamy Chicken Gravy, and festive vegetables—Spiced Sweet-potato Bake, Creamed Onions With Peanuts, and broccoli with lemon slices—are traditional holiday fare.

The King's Arms Tavern has been reconstructed on its original foundations on the Duke of Gloucester Street in restored Williamsburg. It stands ready to serve food of the finest quality prepared by old and approved recipes. The moment you are seated at the candlelighted table a waiter in breeches is tying a yard-square linen napkin around your neck. Notice the table appointments. China, silver, and glass are in reproductions of Colonial table fittings. Water glasses are hand blown, knives have pistol handles, and the forks are three-tined.

CHICKEN PYES

1 5-pound stewing chicken, cut up
5 cups water
1 onion
2 stalks celery
1 teaspoon salt
¼ cup chicken fat
¼ cup all-purpose flour
2 cups chicken broth
½ teaspoon salt
4 cups diced cooked chicken
Double recipe plain pastry

Simmer chicken in water with onion, celery, and salt until tender, about 3 hours. Let chicken cool to room temperature in broth; skim off fat. Remove chicken meat from the bones and cut in cubes.

Melt chicken fat; blend in flour. Add broth gradually and cook until thick, stirring constantly. Add salt and chicken; cool. Spoon mixture into five 5-inch pastry-lined piepans. Make 7 slashes in each top crust, radiating outward from center. Adjust top crusts; crimp edges. Bake in hot oven (400°) about 30 minutes or till golden brown. Remove from pans before serving.

Serve with *Creamy Chicken Gravy:* Melt ¼ cup chicken fat; add ⅓ cup all-purpose flour. Gradually stir in 1 cup milk and 1 cup chicken broth. Cook until thick, stirring constantly. Add ¼ teaspoon salt and dash of white pepper. Makes 5 servings.

CREAMED ONIONS WITH PEANUTS

16 small white onions
2 tablespoons butter or margarine
2 tablespoons all-purpose flour
2 cups milk
¼ teaspoon salt
½ cup buttered bread crumbs
⅓ cup chopped peanuts

Cook onions in boiling salted water till tender; drain. Melt butter; stir in flour. Add milk gradually; cook until thick, stirring constantly. Add salt. Place hot onions in 1-quart casserole. Pour sauce over. Combine crumbs and peanuts; sprinkle atop. Bake in 400° oven 10 minutes. Serves 4 to 5.

SPICED SWEET-POTATO BAKE

3 pounds sweet potatoes
½ cup sugar
3 tablespoons butter or margarine
½ teaspoon *each* cinnamon, and nutmeg
¼ teaspoon salt
About 1 cup milk

Cook sweet potatoes in boiling salted water till tender, about 15 minutes. Peel and mash. Add sugar, butter, spices, and salt. Add enough milk to moisten. Put in buttered 1½-quart casserole; sprinkle with sugar. Bake at 400° for 30 minutes. Serves 8 to 10.

HOLIDAY EGGNOG

¼ cup sugar
¼ teaspoon *each* cinnamon, ginger, and cloves
6 well-beaten eggs
2 quarts orange juice, chilled
½ cup lemon juice, chilled
1 quart vanilla ice cream
1 quart ginger ale, chilled

Beat sugar and spices into beaten eggs. Stir in chilled orange and lemon juices. Cut ice cream in chunks; put in punch bowl. Pour ginger ale over ice cream. Then stir in egg mixture. Sprinkle with nutmeg. Serves 20.

Christmas dinner begins in elegant style at Williamsburg —a scoop of raspberry sherbet on a chilled grapefruit half.

BRUNSWICK STEW

1 5- to 6-pound stewing chicken, cut up
8 cups water
1 teaspoon salt
1 10-ounce package frozen (2 cups) baby Lima beans
1 1-pound 13-ounce can (3½ cups) tomatoes
2 large onions, sliced (about 2 cups)
2½ cups diced potatoes (about 4 medium)
1 1-pound can (2 cups) sliced okra
2 1-pound cans (4 cups) whole kernel corn, drained
1 teaspoon salt
½ teaspoon pepper
1 tablespoon sugar

Place chicken in Dutch oven or deep kettle. Add water and 1 teaspoon salt. Cover and simmer (*do not boil*) till tender, about 2½ hours. Cool chicken in broth. Remove meat from bones. Skim fat from broth.

Add remaining ingredients except chicken to broth; cover and simmer 1 hour. Add cut up chicken, salt and pepper. Heat mixture through. Ladle into soup bowls and serve piping hot. Makes 8 to 10 servings.

SALLY LUNN

1 package active dry yeast
¼ cup warm water
¾ cup milk, scalded
3 tablespoons butter or margarine
3 tablespoons sugar
2 eggs
3½ cups sifted all-purpose flour
1¼ teaspoons salt

Soften yeast in water. Cool milk to lukewarm; add to yeast mixture and set aside.

Cream butter and sugar; add eggs one at a time, beating after each. Add flour and salt to creamed mixture alternately with yeast mixture, beating well after each addition. Beat till smooth. Cover and let rise till double, about 1 hour.

Beat down and pour into a well greased Sally Lunn Mold or a 10-inch tube pan. Let rise till double, about 30 minutes. Bake in a moderate oven (350°) for 40 to 45 minutes or till golden brown and crusty. Serve hot.

WILLIAMSBURG LODGE SANDWICH

Toast 3 slices white bread for each sandwich. Butter toast. On bottom slice, place layer of Chicken Salad, Williamsburg-style. Sprinkle with chopped parsley or shredded lettuce. Add second slice of toast; spread with mayonnaise, and cover with thin tomato and avocado slices. Top with third slice of toast. Anchor with 4 toothpicks. Trim off crusts. Cut sandwich criss-cross into fourths. Garnish with parsley if desired.

CHICKEN SALAD, WILLIAMSBURG-STYLE

Combine 1½ cups diced cooked chicken, 1½ cups chopped celery, and 2 hard-cooked egg whites, chopped. Toss with chilled *Dressing, Williamsburg-style:* Beat 2 egg yolks till lemon-colored; beat in ¼ cup vinegar or lemon juice gradually. Stir over hot water until mixture thickens. Remove from heat. Slowly beat in ½ teaspoon sugar, ¾ teaspoon salt, ⅛ teaspoon cayenne pepper, 2 teaspoons prepared mustard. Cool. Gradually beat in ¼ cup olive oil. Beat till smooth. Chill. Combine with chicken mixture. Spread on first layer of toast for Williamsburg Lodge Sandwich. Fills 6 to 8 sandwiches.

SPOONBREAD

1 cup cornmeal
1⅓ cups boiling water
1 tablespoon sugar
1 tablespoon baking powder
1 teaspoon salt
¼ cup butter or margarine
1⅓ cups milk
3 well beaten egg yolks
3 stiffly beaten egg whites

Cook and stir cornmeal and water until the consistency of mush. Remove mixture from heat; add sugar, baking powder, salt, and butter. Stir in milk and well beaten egg yolks. Fold in stiff beaten egg whites. Bake in a greased 2-quart casserole in a slow oven (325°) for 50 to 55 minutes. Serve while hot. Makes 8 servings.

WHITE FRUITCAKE

1 cup butter or margarine
1 cup sugar
6 large eggs (1⅓ cups)
2 cups sifted all-purpose flour
1½ teaspoons baking powder
1 teaspoon salt
¼ teaspoon nutmeg
Dash mace
½ cup orange juice
1½ cups white raisins
1 cup chopped candied citron
⅓ cup chopped candied pineapple
⅓ cup candied cherries, cut in half
1 cup slivered, blanched almonds
1½ cups shredded coconut

Cream butter to soften; then thoroughly cream butter and sugar till fluffy; beat in eggs. Sift together flour, baking powder, salt, and spices; stir into creamed mixture alternately with the orange juice.
Stir in fruits, nuts, and coconut. Line 9½x 5x3-inch loaf pan with heavy brown paper; grease. Spoon in batter. Bake in slow oven (300°) for 2½ to 3 hours or until done. Cover with paper the last hour of baking.

CAKE SQUARES

½ cup shortening
1 cup sugar
1 teaspoon vanilla
2 cups sifted cake flour
2½ teaspoons baking powder
¾ teaspoon salt
1 cup milk minus 2 tablespoons
3 stiffly beaten egg whites
¼ cup sugar

Thoroughly cream shortening and 1 cup sugar; add vanilla. Sift together flour, baking powder, and salt; add alternately with milk to creamed mixture. Mix well after each addition. Beat egg whites until foamy; gradually add ¼ cup sugar, beating just to soft peaks. Fold egg whites into batter. Bake in greased 11x7x1½-inch pan in 375° oven about 30 minutes. Cool; frost with Butter Cream Frosting. Cut in squares.

Butter Cream Frosting: Thoroughly cream ⅓ cup butter or margarine and 2 cups sifted confectioners' sugar. Add 2 tablespoons cooking sherry; beat well. Add 1 teaspoon grated orange peel and 1 egg white; beat till mixture is of spreading consistency.

Serve Virginia ham, plain, in all its glory, on buttered slices of French bread, the way they do at Colonial Williamsburg. It has the wonderful and distinctive flavor obtained with long curing and smoking in the traditional fashion of this section of the country. Delicious.

Try these two favorite desserts from the Williamsburg Inn. Fresh Fruit Ambrosia bedecked with bright maraschino cherries and mint; luscious three-layer Coconut Cake with a rich buttery flavor.

COCONUT CAKE

¾ cup butter or margarine
2¼ cups sugar
1½ teaspoons vanilla
3 eggs
3¼ cups sifted cake flour
4 teaspoons baking powder
1½ teaspoons salt
1½ cups milk

Cream butter to soften; gradually add sugar; cream thoroughly. Add vanilla. Beat in eggs, one at a time, beating till fluffy. Sift together flour, baking powder, and salt; add to creamed mixture alternately with milk beginning and ending with flour mixture. Beat after each addition. Turn into 3 paper-lined 9x1½-inch round cake pans. Bake in a 375° oven 20 to 25 minutes. Cool and frost.

Coconut Frosting: Combine 1½ cups sugar, ½ cup water, and ¼ teaspoon cream of tartar in saucepan. Bring to a boil, stirring constantly. Cover pan 2 to 3 minutes to dissolve sugar crystals on side of pan. Uncover; cook to hard ball stage (266°). Gradually add hot syrup to 4 stiffly beaten egg whites, beating constantly. Add 1 teaspoon vanilla; beat till frosting is of spreading consistency. Add ½ cup coconut to frosting. Spread on cake; sprinkle top and sides with 1 cup shredded coconut.

FRESH FRUIT AMBROSIA

3 large oranges
1 fresh ripe pineapple
1 cup shredded coconut
¾ cup sugar
Dash salt

Pare oranges with a sharp knife; remove sections by cutting close to membrane. Pare, core, and dice the pineapple. Combine fruit with coconut, sugar, and salt; toss lightly. Chill several hours. Spoon in serving bowl and decorate top with additional orange sections, coconut, and a few maraschino cherries and mint leaves. Makes 6 servings.

FISH CHOWDER

1 cup diced potato
¾ cup diced onion

• • •

1 ounce (¼ cup) cubed salt pork
1¼ pounds boned haddock, cut in ¼-inch cubes
2 cups water
2 to 3 cups light cream
Salt and pepper to taste

Put potato and onion through food chopper, using coarse blade. Fry salt pork till lightly browned. Place alternate layers of potato mixture and the fish in a deep kettle. Add salt pork and water. Cover and bake in hot oven (400°) for 15 minutes, then in moderate oven (350°) 45 minutes—or cover and simmer over low heat for 1 hour. Add cream; season to taste with salt and pepper, and heat thoroughly. Garnish with chopped chives, if desired. Makes 6 to 8 servings.

HARTWELL FARM CORN PUDDING

1 1-pound can (2 cups) cream-style corn
1 cup medium-fine dry bread crumbs
1 cup milk
2 tablespoons chopped green pepper
1 teaspoon salt
¼ teaspoon pepper

• • •

4 ounces sliced Cheddar cheese, cut in 1½-inch squares
3 slices bacon, cut in 1½-inch lengths

Combine cream-style corn, bread crumbs, milk, green pepper, salt, and pepper; mix well. Pour mixture into a 10x6x2-inch baking dish. Arrange alternate pieces of Cheddar cheese and bacon across the top in checkerboard fashion. Bake pudding in slow oven (325°) for about 1 to 1¼ hours or until done. Makes 4 to 6 servings.

LINCOLN

Hartwell Farm

Situated on Concord Road where Redcoats tramped during Revolution times, the Hartwell Farm dates from 1636. Marion Fitch (present owner) and the late Jane Poor made the house into a restaurant that keeps the charm of those olden days. Shelves of antiques line the walls, and at one end of the dining room is a crescent-shaped table facing the fireplace. A perfect spot for party dinners, the table is designed so everyone can watch the cheery, crackling fire while dining.

The food at Hartwell Farm is descended from yesteryear's grand New England cookery. On a cold evening, treat your family to their Fish Chowder supper. It's a substantial dish with the homey flavors of salt pork and onion blended through. At Hartwell Farm chowder is served in a soup crock (see picture), and diners help themselves, then dress their salads from cruets and little crock jars. Hartwell Farm Corn Pudding is the kind of satisfying vegetable dish that old-time New England cooks proudly took to Grange suppers, and coffee-flavored Chocolate Sauce is perfect for making sundaes or lacing over ice cream pies.

CHOCOLATE SAUCE

4 1-ounce squares unsweetened chocolate
⅔ cup strong coffee
1 cup sugar
¼ teaspoon salt

Combine the chocolate and coffee in a small saucepan; cook, stirring constantly, over low heat until chocolate melts and mixture is smooth. Stir in sugar and salt; cook, stirring constantly, until sugar dissolves. Makes about 1½ cups sauce.

ABNER

FRAMINGHAM

Abner Wheeler House

Host-owner Frank R. Gustie has made this Massachusetts country mansion into a restaurant famed for New England foods. In the Antique Room shown at left, you may dine within sight of a fireplace well over 200 years old. Heavy long-handled pans and skillets, once essential to open-fire cooking, show the scars of having been used well before they became a part of the decor. Pewter ware is reminiscent of days when America blended the food customs of many lands.

Foods served at Abner Wheeler House are those that have become an important part of traditional American foods. Cranberry sauce and jellies, Thanksgiving Turkey Stuffing, Baked Indian Pudding, or Pecan Pie borrowed from Southern friends are dishes not to be separated from thoughts of early New England life. Fish and sea food naturally account for a large part of the menu. Favorites from nearby bays and sounds include lobster, shrimp, and scrod.

Built in 1721 by local Framingham politician Abner Wheeler, this mansion has seen many changes during the last two centuries. At one time the house became a haven for artists. Rooms have been added at various times, and today five private rooms add to the space available in the main dining room and lounge. Mr. Gustie has preserved an Early American flavor in the Abner Wheeler House, not only through the display of his collected antiques, but also through the excellent quality of food and the friendly service he offers.

BAKED INDIAN PUDDING

4 cups milk
½ cup yellow corn meal

• • •

½ teaspoon salt
½ teaspoon mace or cinnamon
¼ teaspoon ginger
¼ teaspoon cloves, if desired
¼ teaspoon nutmeg, if desired
2 tablespoons butter or margarine
¾ cup light molasses
1 beaten egg
2 cups milk

• • •

Vanilla ice cream

Pour 4 cups milk in the top of a double boiler; gradually stir in corn meal. Cook over boiling water stirring frequently, until mixture is thick, about 10 to 15 minutes. Add salt, mace or cinnamon, ginger, cloves, nutmeg, butter, molasses, beaten egg, and 2 cups milk; mix well. Pour mixture into a 2-quart casserole and bake in a very slow oven (250°) for 5 hours. Cool until pudding is just slightly warm. To serve, spoon into sauce dishes and top with vanilla ice cream curls. Make ice cream curls by scraping about ⅛ inch deep across the surface of ice cream with the tip of a teaspoon. Makes 8 servings.

GARLIC DRESSING

1½ cups salad oil
2 tablespoons lemon juice
2 tablespoons vinegar

• • •

2 tablespoons finely chopped onion
1½ teaspoons salt
1 teaspoon Worcestershire sauce
Dash white pepper
2 drops bottled hot pepper sauce
2 cloves garlic, minced

Combine salad oil, lemon juice, and vinegar in a bottle or jar. Add onion, salt, Worcestershire, white pepper, hot pepper sauce, and garlic; cover tightly. Let stand at least 6 to 8 hours for flavors to blend. Shake dressing well before using. Serve over crisp green salad. Makes about 2 cups dressing.

ABNER WHEELER HOUSE PECAN PIE

1½ cups sifted all-purpose flour
½ teaspoon salt
½ cup shortening
4 to 5 tablespoons cold water

• • •

2 tablespoons soft butter or margarine
¼ cup brown sugar
½ cup sifted all-purpose flour
3 cups light corn syrup
1 teaspoon vanilla
Dash salt
3 beaten eggs
1 cup pecan halves

Sift together flour and ½ teaspoon salt. Cut in shortening till pieces are the size of small peas. Add water, 1 tablespoon at a time, tossing gently till flour mixture is moistened. Gather into a ball with fingers. On a lightly floured surface, flatten ball slightly; roll to ⅛ inch thickness. Transfer to 9-inch pie plate. Fit loosely onto bottom and sides. Trim ½ to 1 inch beyond edge; fold under and flute.

Cream butter and brown sugar; stir in flour, syrup, vanilla, and salt. Add beaten eggs and mix well. Pour filling into unbaked pie shell; sprinkle pecan halves over top. Bake in a moderate oven (350°) for about 1 hour and 10 minutes, or until knife inserted halfway between outside and center of filling comes out clean. Cool before serving.

THANKSGIVING TURKEY STUFFING

½ pound salt pork, diced
1½ cups diced onion
1 1-pound loaf day-old white bread, finely crumbed (8 cups)
⅔ cup chopped pecans
1 teaspoon poultry seasoning
1 teaspoon salt
¼ teaspoon pepper

Fry diced pork and onion together until lightly browned. Add bread crumbs, nuts, and seasonings. Makes 9 cups stuffing, or enough for a 10- to 12-pound turkey.

SOUTH SUDBURY

Longfellow's Wayside Inn

In 1716 this Early American Massachusetts inn was properly licensed by the Concord Court to be a "hous of entertainment for travelers." Since then many a traveler has found food, lodging, and drink in accord with old colonial laws. Originally named the Red Horse Tavern, Henry Wadsworth Longfellow's impressions of its warm hospitality inspired his now famous "Tales of a Wayside Inn."

YANKEE BEAN SOUP

½ pound (1¼ cups) dried navy beans
½ teaspoon salt
1 teaspoon molasses
2 ounces (½ cup) salt pork, cut in ¼-inch cubes
⅓ cup onion rings
3 slices bacon, cut in pieces
¼ cup chopped onion
½ cup diced cooked carrot
⅓ cup finely chopped celery leaves
1 teaspoon molasses
2 cups milk

Add 5 cups water to beans. Bring to boiling; remove from heat and let stand at least 2 hours. Add next 4 ingredients. Simmer covered 2 hours or till beans are tender; stir occasionally. Cook bacon and *chopped* onion just till bacon is lightly brown. Mash beans slightly; add bacon, remaining ingredients, and salt to taste. Simmer 10 minutes, stirring occasionally. Serves 4 to 6.

HOT MULLED CIDER

Combine ½ cup brown sugar, ¼ teaspoon salt, and 2 quarts cider. Tie 1 teaspoon *each* whole allspice and whole cloves, 3 inches stick cinnamon, and a dash nutmeg in cheesecloth. Add to cider. Slowly bring to boiling; simmer, covered, 20 minutes. Serve immediately. Makes about 10 servings.

TOLL HOUSE PANCAKES

1 cup sifted all-purpose flour
2 teaspoons sugar
¾ teaspoon baking powder
¼ teaspoon salt

. . .

1¼ cups buttermilk
½ teaspoon soda
2 beaten egg yolks

. . .

2 tablespoons soft butter
or margarine
2 stiff-beaten egg whites

. . .

1 recipe Chicken Filling and
Mushroom Sauce
Grated Parmesan cheese

Sift together flour, sugar, baking powder, and salt. Beat buttermilk and soda into the egg yolks with a rotary beater, or use an electric mixer at low speed. Add dry ingredients and softened butter. Beat just until smooth, then fold in the egg whites.

Drop batter from the tip of spoon onto hot, greased griddle to make 5-inch pancakes. When tops are bubbly and a few bubbles have broken, turn cakes and cook on other side. (Keep pancakes warm between towels on a baking sheet in very slow oven.)

Put 1 tablespoon Chicken Filling on each pancake and roll up. Place pancakes, edges down in an 11½x7½x1½-inch baking dish. Pour the Mushroom Sauce over and sprinkle with grated Parmesan cheese. Broil at low heat until golden. Makes 4 servings.

WHITMAN

Toll House

"Welcome to gracious dining and warm hospitality" reads the door mat at the Toll House, just 40 miles south of Boston in Whitman, Massachusetts. Here, in a lovely country eating place with garden terrace, spacious lawns, restful pools, and old apple trees, visitors are served in the old New England style.

Guests have a choice of dining in several rooms—the large garden room built around a huge old elm tree, the terrace, or the more private, quaint upstairs rooms. In 1709 early travelers ate here while the coachman paid the toll and changed horses. Today people flock to the dining rooms to enjoy the excellent cooking and beautiful table settings. Unusual china, linens, and glassware, brought from all over the world by the Wakefields (owners), grace each table.

Here we show a favorite luncheon dish—delicate Toll House Pancakes generously filled with a tasty Chicken Filling and topped with rich Mushroom Sauce and a sprinkling of grated Parmesan cheese.

CHICKEN FILLING AND MUSHROOM SAUCE

- 3 tablespoons butter or margarine
- 3 tablespoons all-purpose flour
- ½ teaspoon salt
- 1⅓ cups chicken broth
- 1 cup ½-inch cubes cooked chicken
- ⅓ cup sliced mushrooms
- 2 teaspoons butter or margarine
- 3 tablespoons light cream

For Chicken Filling, melt 3 tablespoons butter; blend in flour and salt. Add chicken broth all at once; cook, stirring constantly, until mixture thickens and boils. Cook 2 minutes longer. Reserve half this sauce for Mushroom Sauce; to other half of sauce add cubed chicken and mix well. Heat through.

For Mushroom Sauce, cook mushrooms in 2 teaspoons butter until tender; add to reserved sauce. Stir in cream; heat through. Serve over Toll House Pancakes.

Crusty, delicious Baked Stuffed Shrimp with hot drawn butter makes a tempting luncheon dish. Served with it are a basket of Yankee Corn Sticks and broccoli topped with Cheddar Cheese Sauce.

Boston Cream Pie remains a sweet tradition at the Publick House. Fluffy, light sponge cake layers sandwich in a velvety cream filling, then a luscious chocolate glaze goes over all—a delicious dessert!

STURBRIDGE

Publick House

Old-fashioned as the spinning wheel in the hallway, yet modern as the thermostat above it on the wall—that's the Publick House. This gracious Colonial inn was founded by Col. Ebenezer Crafts in 1771 as a coaching tavern. Now one of the Treadway Inns, it is a wonderful combination of the old and the new, and offers sumptuous New England meals and overnight hospitality.

Folks who spend the night at the inn find a surprise snack on the bedside table—two crisp, rosy apples along with a paring knife. In the morning they awaken to the village church bell. At the same time the grandfather's clock at the foot of the stairs chimes away, and the tantalizing aroma of sizzling bacon and griddle cakes drifts up from the kitchen.

The Publick House itself is in the little town of Sturbridge, Massachusetts, 60 miles out of Boston. Just down the road a piece is Old Sturbridge Village, a 200-acre museum town of homes, shops, and mills—complete with meeting house and village green. Here time turns back a century and a half as visitors set out afoot or by horse and wagon to see how rural New Englanders lived in the early 1800s. Costumed attendants weave, shoe horses, run the grist mills, and bake in the great brick ovens. Every place in the village hums with activity.

Mealtime at the Publick House also brings together the old and new. Whatever you choose—from grilled tenderloin or Red Caviar Omelet to broiled Maine lobster or Baked Stuffed Shrimp—you can round out your meal with country-kitchen specials. For example, an appetizer of New England Clam Chowder, a dessert of chocolate-glazed Boston Cream Pie, a basket of hot Yankee Corn Sticks—these are heirloom recipes and Yankee cooking at its very best.

Red Caviar Omelet is a gourmet's dish. The exotic tang of red caviar and the tartness of sour cream contrast deliciously with the delicate French Omelet. Iced melon with lime sherbet is the appetizer.

Come chilly weather, New England Corn Chowder is a popular steaming-hot bracer. It's pleasingly hearty, and flavored with bacon bits and onion. The floaters are water biscuits, split and toasted.

BAKED STUFFED SHRIMP

- 12 jumbo shrimp (about 5 inches long)
- ½ pound scallops
- ¼ cup butter or margarine, melted
- ¼ teaspoon paprika
- 2 tablespoons crushed potato chips
- ¼ cup cracker meal
- 3 tablespoons grated Parmesan cheese

With sharp knife cut shrimp from underside through meat but not through shell; wash and devein. Put toothpick under meat, but over shell, at both ends to keep flat during baking. Chop raw scallops and fill into shrimp. Combine butter and paprika in saucepan; cook over very slow heat 10 minutes to take raw taste out of paprika. Combine with potato chips, cracker meal, and Parmesan. Cover shrimp with this mixture; place in shallow baking dish with a little water in the bottom to prevent drying. Bake in moderate oven (350°) for about 20 to 25 minutes. If desired, sprinkle 1 to 2 tablespoons cooking sherry over the shrimp just before removing from oven. Serve shrimp with lemon wedges. Makes 4 servings.

CHEDDAR CHEESE SAUCE

Melt 2 tablespoons butter; blend in 2 tablespoons flour. Add 1 cup milk; cook and stir till mixture comes to boil. Remove from heat; add 1 cup grated Cheddar cheese; stir till melted. Stir in 1 slightly beaten egg; cook and stir a minute or two. Season to taste with salt and pepper.

YANKEE CORN STICKS

- 1⅓ cups sifted all-purpose flour
- ⅔ cup corn meal
- 2 teaspoons baking powder
- ½ teaspoon salt
- 3 tablespoons sugar
- 1 well-beaten egg
- ⅔ cup cream-style canned corn
- 1 cup milk
- 2 tablespoons salad oil

Sift together dry ingredients. Combine egg, corn, milk, and oil; mix well. Add to dry mixture; stir just till moistened—don't beat. Fill well-greased heated corn-stick pans. Bake at 425° for 20 minutes. Makes 12.

BOSTON CREAM PIE

1 cup sugar
1 cup sifted cake flour
5 eggs, separated
½ teaspoon salt
1 teaspoon grated lemon peel
1 tablespoon lemon juice
1 recipe Pastry Cream
1 recipe Chocolate Glaze

Add ¼ *cup of the* sugar to flour; sift together 4 times. Beat egg *whites* till foamy; add salt; beat till stiff (not dry) peaks form. Beat in remaining sugar, 2 tablespoons at a time. Beat yolks till thick and lemon-colored; add lemon peel and juice. Fold whites into yolks. Sift ¼ the flour mixture over top of egg mixture; gently fold in. Repeat till all flour is blended in. Carefully pour into 2 paper-lined 9x1½-inch round cake pans; tap on table once to break any large air bubbles. Bake in moderate oven (350°) for about 25 minutes or till done. Cool. Fill with Pastry Cream; top with Chocolate Glaze.

PASTRY CREAM

2 egg yolks
¼ cup sugar
¼ cup all-purpose flour
Dash salt
1 cup milk, scalded
1 teaspoon vanilla
¼ cup whipping cream, whipped

Beat yolks with wire whisk. Beat in sugar, then flour and salt. Add scalded milk, stirring constantly. Cook and stir over low heat till mixture thickens. Remove; add vanilla. Cool. Fold in whipped cream.

CHOCOLATE GLAZE

1 1-ounce square unsweetened chocolate
1 tablespoon butter
½ cup sifted confectioners' sugar
1 tablespoon milk

Melt chocolate and butter in double boiler over *hot, not boiling water.* Remove from heat; add sugar and milk; blend till smooth.

RED CAVIAR OMELET WITH SOUR CREAM

Garnish top of a folded French Omelet with a band of red caviar (as much as you can afford). Beside it, spoon on a band of dairy sour cream. Trim with parsley sprigs.

FRENCH OMELET

The pan should be of heavy metal and at least 6 inches across for an individual omelet. Preheat pan for about 10 minutes over very low heat. For each omelet beat 3 eggs, 1 tablespoon water, and dash salt with a fork or a rotary beater until well blended but not frothy; strain. When ready to make omelet, turn up heat under pan. (The pan should be hot enough to make butter sizzle but not brown.) Put a good tablespoon butter in the pan and when it is melted, pour in the eggs. Leave for about 30 seconds, until the bottom starts to set a little, then shake the pan with one hand and stir the eggs lightly with a fork with the other hand. While the omelet is still soft and creamy, let stand for a few seconds, then tilt the pan at right angles toward a hot plate or omelet dish, and with same fork, fold the omelet over and turn out onto the plate.

NEW ENGLAND CORN CHOWDER

4 slices bacon
1 medium onion, thinly sliced
2 cups water
2 cups diced potatoes
Salt, pepper
2 cups cream-style corn (1 1-pound can)
2 cups light cream
1 tablespoon butter

Cook bacon in saucepan till some of fat is fried out. Add onion; cook till bacon is crisp and onions lightly browned. Remove bacon; drain on paper towels. (Remove excess fat from saucepan.) Add water, potatoes, salt, and pepper to saucepan; cover and simmer 20 minutes. Add corn and cream; simmer 5 minutes longer. Crumble the bacon; just before serving, add bacon bits and butter to corn mixture. Makes 6 to 8 servings.

ROAST WHOLE BONELESS CHICKEN

2 2- to 2½-pound ready-to-cook broiler-fryer chickens

• • •

½ pound (1½ cups) wild rice
½ 5-ounce can (¼ cup) pâté de foie gras
½ cup brandy
½ teaspoon salt
Dash white pepper

• • •

2 tablespoons butter, melted
2 tablespoons all-purpose flour
1½ teaspoons lemon juice
1½ cups chicken stock
2 slightly beaten egg yolks

• • •

1 cup seedless white grapes

Have meatman bone chickens, or do it yourself, using very sharp knife: Remove wings and neck. Cut through skin along backbone. With back of chicken toward you, begin at tail and start cutting meat away from backbone and ribs on one side. Turn chicken around and start cutting from the neck until you have both sides cut loose from the bones. Lay chicken flat on a cutting board, push thigh meat down to drumstick joint, sever at joint and take bones out of both thighs, leaving the drumsticks in.

For *Wild-rice Stuffing:* Cook wild rice according to package directions; drain. Mix rice with pâté de foie gras, brandy, salt, and pepper. Stuff chickens; skewer closed.

Place on rack in shallow roasting pan; brush generously with melted butter. Roast uncovered at 325° for 1¼ hours or until tender, basting with pan drippings. When chicken is almost done, make Sauce Veronica.

Sauce Veronica: Blend flour into melted butter; add lemon juice, then gradually stir in chicken stock. Cook and stir until sauce thickens and bubbles. Stir small amount hot mixture into egg yolks; return to hot mixture, and cook, stirring constantly, just until sauce begins to bubble. Season to taste with salt and pepper. Stir in white grapes. Makes about 2 cups gravy. Serve hot over chicken. Makes 2 servings.

ATLANTA

Hart's Peachtree

Elegance reigns in the gray stone mansion-turned-restaurant, known as Hart's Peachtree, on historic Peachtree Road in Atlanta. Keeping his philosophy in mind that "good food cannot be hurried," the continental Mr. William Hart strives for perfection in cuisine and service and for an atmosphere of gracious, intimate and relaxed dining in his restaurant.

Today, with the same cooks he himself trained in the beginning, Mr. Hart offers as cosmopolitan a menu as you will find anywhere. Each dish is perfectly seasoned and beautifully served.

At left, Mr. Hart presents two superb choices. Delectable Roast Whole Boneless Chicken with Wild-rice Stuffing and delicate Sauce Veronica grace the silver platter in the foreground. The Rich Tenderloin Tips in Burgundy Wine a la Deutsch, bordered with German fried potatoes, fill the chafing dish. For dessert, he suggests Key lime chiffon pie or peaches Melba.

TENDERLOIN TIPS IN BURGUNDY WINE A LA DEUTSCH

6 tablespoons butter or margarine
1½ pounds beef tenderloin, cut in very thin 2- to 3-inch strips
½ teaspoon salt
2 medium-sized onions, chopped
2 green peppers, chopped
1¼ cups brown beef gravy or 1 can brown gravy
1 cup red Burgundy wine
2 tablespoons cornstarch

Melt 2 tablespoons of the butter in skillet. Sprinkle beef with salt. Sauteing a third of meat at one time, brown strips quickly all over, then remove from pan—add 2 tablespoons butter as needed. Add remaining butter to empty skillet; saute vegetables for about 3 minutes. Add gravy. Slowly stir wine into cornstarch; then stir into gravy mixture. Cook and stir till mixture bubbles; cook and stir 2 minutes longer. Season with salt and pepper. Add browned beef; heat through. Just before serving, border with German fried potatoes. Serves 6.

WHITE SULPHUR SPRINGS

Greenbrier

Gaze out the windows in any of The Greenbrier dining rooms and you'll glory in the same vistas and mountain scenery as have many of our history's venerables. To White Sulphur Springs, West Virginia, came Daniel Webster and Henry Clay, General Robert E. Lee, and Jefferson Davis—and at least 16 presidents of the United States including former President Eisenhower.

Piazza-fronted white brick cottages line Paradise Row where pleasure seekers of the early 1800s lived. Across the threshold of The President's Cottage, now a museum, John Tyler ("Tippecanoe and Tyler too") carried his beautiful Virginia bride. In these cottages and in The Greenbrier itself, artful color schemes and furnishings are planned by Decorator Dorothy Draper.

Vice President E. Truman Wright directs the magnificent Greenbrier. Built and owned by the Chesapeake & Ohio Railway, The Greenbrier is often fondly called "The Old White" after its predecessor which was the first big hotel in White Sulphur Springs. Here Southern hospitality has the same warmth as in olden times. And no one is more responsible for the guests' delight than Executive Food Director Herman G. Rusch. He is one of the "Order of the Golden Dozen," composed of the world's 12 greatest chefs. Name any honor in culinary circles and he'll probably already have it! Many of his large staff of chefs are award winners in their own right.

At left a Greenbrier chef stands ready to serve Baked Smithfield Ham Gourmet, Greenbrier Beef Stroganoff, noodles, Tomato Florentine, and Southern Biscuits from a buffet table in the Cameo Ballroom. Ice carvings such as the one shown at the right of the table are often displayed. This traditional form of art is taught in the Greenbrier's own culinary school.

Each year White Sulphur Springs celebrates the coming of Spring with a festival. A high light of the festival is the annual Anniversary Ball held in the Cameo Ballroom. Here the Duke and Duchess of Windsor once won the waltz contest when the hotel was reopened after World War II.

Strawberry time! On table: Southern Strawberry Meringue Tart, Aloha Salads. First tray: Strawberries Supreme. Top: Strawberry Parfait Royale.

TOMATO FLORENTINE

6 medium-sized tomatoes
Salt
½ cup light cream
1 egg yolk
12 ounces fresh spinach, cooked, chopped, and drained (¾ cup drained)
3 tablespoons butter, melted

Cut top (¼ inch) off each tomato. Empty inside completely of juice and seeds, but not fruit. Sprinkle inside with salt. Combine cream and egg yolk; add chopped spinach and *1 tablespoon* of the butter. Salt to taste. Heat and stir *just* to simmering. Fill tomatoes solid with the creamed spinach. Place in a 10x6-inch baking dish. Top each with *1 teaspoon* melted butter. Bake at 375° for 20 minutes. Serve hot. Makes 6 servings.

BAKED SMITHFIELD HAM GOURMET

Order a Smithfield or Virginia ham. Scrub in warm water, using a stiff brush to remove excess pepper. Soak, skin up, in cold water to cover for 24 hours (or follow soaking schedule that comes with ham). Place ham skin down in a big, deep roaster and add fresh cold water to cover completely; simmer 5 to 6 hours (or according to label directions). Cool in the broth. Just before ham is cold, remove skin carefully so as not to tear fat. Now cut crisscross lines in the fat; stick a clove into each lozenge of fat. Sieve brown sugar evenly over surface. Bake in shallow pan (no rack) in moderate oven (375°) 20 minutes. Baste with ginger ale; bake 30 to 45 minutes longer, basting frequently with ginger ale and checking to see when ham is enrobed with a golden brown coating. Chill before slicing. Slice tissue-paper thin. To match picture, garnish with maraschino cherries in centers of canned apricots. Secure with toothpicks.

GREENBRIER BEEF STROGANOFF

1 pound lean beef filet
1 tablespoon paprika
3 tablespoons olive oil
4 ounces mushrooms, sliced
1 cup white cooking sherry
½ cup beef stock or canned condensed beef broth
1 cup dairy sour cream
1 teaspoon lemon juice
Salt to taste
Fine noodles, cooked

Cut beef in ¼-inch-thick strips; add paprika. Heat olive oil, then saute the beef very fast (2 to 4 minutes). Take meat from pan. Add mushrooms and saute a few minutes; remove. Then add sherry to pan; reduce to one-half its volume by boiling. Add beef stock and let boil briskly (uncovered) 5 minutes. Add sour cream, lemon juice, and salt to taste. Now add the meat and mushrooms and bring just to boil (do not let boil when meat is in the sauce). Spoon over fine noodles (well-drained and hot). Serves 4.

SOUTHERN STRAWBERRY MERINGUE TART

½ cup butter or margarine, softened
¼ cup sugar
¼ teaspoon salt
1 egg
1½ cups sifted all-purpose flour

• • •

¼ cup sugar
5 teaspoons cornstarch
Dash salt
1 cup milk
2 slightly beaten egg yolks
½ teaspoon vanilla
6 cups hulled whole strawberries

• • •

Strawberry Glaze
Meringue Topping

Cream butter with ¼ cup sugar and ¼ teaspoon salt. Stir in egg and flour. Chill slightly. On lightly floured surface, roll to 12-inch circle. Carefully place dough over *outside* of 9x1½-inch round cake pan. Shape to sides of pan *almost* to rim. (Be sure there are *no thin places* in crust, especially where sides and bottom of pan join.) Trim excess crust. Place pan, with crust up, on baking sheet. Bake at 450° for 8 to 10 minutes or till lightly browned. Cool.

For *Vanilla Cream Filling,* blend ¼ cup sugar, cornstarch, and dash salt. Gradually stir in milk. Bring to boiling, stirring constantly. Reduce heat; cook and stir till thick. Add a little hot mixture to egg yolks; return to hot mixture. Again stirring, bring just to boiling. Add vanilla. Cool. Chill. Pour into baked crust. Reserve 1 cup berries; pile remaining berries atop filling.

Strawberry Glaze: Crush reserved berries; add 1 cup water. Simmer 2 minutes; sieve. Mix ½ cup sugar and 5 teaspoons cornstarch; stir into berry juice. Cook and stir till thick and clear. Tint with red food coloring if desired. Cool to room temperature; pour over berries in crust. Chill till set, about 2 hours. Top with meringue.

Meringue Topping: Beat 3 egg whites till frothy. Gradually add ½ cup sugar, beating till stiff peaks form. Spread over glazed berries, sealing to edge of crust. Brown in very hot oven (450°) for 2 to 3 minutes.

ALOHA SALADS

Cut chilled fresh pineapples in half lengthwise. Hollow out centers. Cut the fruit in small pieces; place in shells. Arrange mandarin orange sections around edge; fill center with whole fresh strawberries. Dash with aromatic bitters. Serve with Orange Dressing, sour cream, cottage cheese, and pecans, (as in 4-compartment dish in picture).

Orange Dressing: Beat 1 8-ounce package softened cream cheese, ¼ cup orange juice, 1 tablespoon grated orange peel, and dash salt till light and fluffy. Whip ½ cup whipping cream; fold in. Makes 2 cups.

STRAWBERRIES SUPREME

Pile red-ripe strawberries in tall, hollow-stemmed sherbets. Drizzle aromatic bitters over till stems are filled. Trim with greens.

STRAWBERRY PARFAIT ROYALE

Almost fill parfait glasses with strawberry ice cream. Add a generous layer of whole strawberries. Top with rosette of whipped cream and a big juicy berry, point up.

CHAMPAGNE COOKIES

1 egg
2 egg yolks
¾ cup sifted confectioners' sugar
¼ teaspoon salt
1½ teaspoons grated orange peel *or*
  1 teaspoon anise seed
¾ cup sifted cake flour
2 egg whites
½ cup sugar

Beat first 5 ingredients until thick and lemon-colored. Fold in flour. Beat egg whites till foamy; gradually add ½ cup sugar, beating till stiff peaks form. Fold into the flour mixture. Press through pastry tube onto paper-covered baking sheets, making round cookies ¾ to 1 inch in diameter—space 1 inch apart. Sprinkle with granulated sugar. Let rest uncovered 4 hours. Bake at 300° for 15 minutes or till tops spring back when lightly touched. Makes about 9½ dozen.

A refreshing luncheon dish, Orange Bowl Mold with Chicken Salad is a Florida citrus delight. The cool, orange gelatin mold hides a center of chicken salad with crunchy toasted almonds added.

Flavorful Broiled Grapefruit originated at Chalet Suzanne over thirty years ago. Cinnamon-sugar and butter broil together to form a spicy brown glaze, then a tender chicken liver is perched atop.

LAKE WALES

Chalet Suzanne

"I'm a great butter and cream girl," Bertha Hinshaw will tell you. "Nothing is too good for my guests!" That's the secret of the superb food served at this famous inn at Lake Wales in central Florida. Some 30 years ago, petite Mrs. Hinshaw, a widow with 2 children, turned her home into an amazing restaurant. Later she added guest cottages for Florida tourists.

Imagination is the trademark of Mrs. Hinshaw's cooking. For example, she keeps on hand a big canister of sugar with grated orange peel in it. This aromatic, orange flavored sugar is sprinkled over pancakes and finds its way into cake frostings and fruit desserts. Vegetables are deliciously different—baked onions might be filled with chicken livers, or fried tomatoes seasoned with salt and sugar, then dipped in flour and browned in butter. With all hot breads, comes a pitcher of orange-blossom honey.

In the dining room, the beautiful dinnerware and furnishings are a result of Mrs. Hinshaw's world travels. The finest china and crystal adorn every table, and each place setting of sterling is of a different design. The menu is a Wedgewood plaque with main dishes etched in script.

Mrs. Hinshaw is especially proud of her soup creations. In fact, they became so popular that her son, Carl, was inspired to market them. Today the soups are available by mail and in food stores throughout this country and abroad.

When it comes to recipes featuring fresh citrus fruits, (such as the ones given here), you just can't top Bertha Hinshaw's. The sunshine-loaded oranges and grapefruit served at the Chalet are carefully selected from their own groves.

ORANGE BOWL MOLD WITH CHICKEN SALAD

2 envelopes (2 tablespoons) unflavored gelatin
1 cup sugar
3½ cups orange juice
½ cup lemon juice
Few drops orange food coloring
2 large oranges, sectioned (white membrane removed)
1 cup chicken salad

Combine gelatin and sugar; add *1 cup* of the orange juice. Heat and stir over medium heat till gelatin and sugar dissolve. Remove from heat; add remaining orange juice and lemon juice. Tint with orange food coloring. Chill till partially set. Pour into four lightly oiled, shallow 1-cup bowls; insert orange sections, spoke-fashion, around sides of bowls. Chill overnight or till very firm.

When firm, with tablespoon, carefully scoop out ¼ cup gelatin from center of each and fill with chicken salad, (omit celery from your favorite chicken salad and add toasted blanched almonds), making top level with gelatin. To loosen from bowls, run knife around edge, invert and cover with towel wrung out of warm water. To serve, garnish with thin avocado slices and green grapes, if desired. Makes 4 servings.

BROILED GRAPEFRUIT

Count on half a large grapefruit for each serving. Have fruit at room temperature so it will be hot through when top is browned. Cut around every section of grapefruit half, close to membrane—fruit should be completely loosened from shell. Cut a hole in center of grapefruit half and fill with 1 to 1½ tablespoons butter. Sprinkle ½ teaspoon sugar over each half, then sprinkle each with 2 tablespoons cinnamon-sugar mixture (1 part cinnamon to 4 parts sugar).

Broil grapefruit on shallow baking pan or jellyroll pan 4 inches from heat about 8 to 10 minutes or just long enough to brown tops and heat bubbling hot. Then, place a cooked chicken liver in center of each grapefruit half and sprinkle lightly with sugar; broil about 2 minutes longer.

CHALET SUZANNE ORANGE WHIP

2 envelopes (2 tablespoons) unflavored gelatin
2 cups sugar
Dash salt

• • •

4 egg yolks
2½ cups orange juice (about 10 medium oranges)
1 teaspoon grated orange peel
2 teaspoons grated lemon peel
3 tablespoons lemon juice (1 lemon)

• • •

1 cup orange sections (white membrane removed), cut in half (3 to 4 medium oranges)

• • •

2 cups whipping cream, whipped

Thoroughly mix gelatin, sugar, and salt in saucepan. Beat together egg yolks and *1 cup* of the orange juice; stir into gelatin mixture. Cook over medium heat, stirring constantly, just until mixture comes to boiling. Remove from heat; stir in orange and lemon peels and remaining juices. Chill, stirring occasionally, until the mixture mounds when dropped from a spoon.

Stir in orange sections. Fold in whipped cream. Pour into a 2-quart mold. Chill until set. Unmold. (To match picture, divide between a 1-quart fluted mold and an 8x1½-inch round cake pan. Unmold fluted mold atop round, flat mold.) Serves 10 to 12.

ORANGE RICE

2 cups water
1 tablespoon grated orange peel
½ cup orange juice
1 teaspoon salt

• • •

1 cup uncooked long-grain rice

Combine water, orange peel, orange juice, and salt; bring to boiling. Stir in rice; return to boiling, then lower heat, cover and cook over *low* heat until tender and liquid is absorbed, about 25 minutes. Serve hot with Curry of Shrimp. Makes 3½ cups.

CURRY OF SHRIMP, SUZANNE

⅓ cup butter or margarine
3 tablespoons all-purpose flour
1 to 2 tablespoons curry powder
½ teaspoon salt
¼ teaspoon paprika
Dash nutmeg
2 cups light cream
3 cups cleaned cooked shrimp
1 tablespoon finely chopped candied ginger
1 tablespoon lemon juice
1 teaspoon cooking sherry
1 teaspoon onion juice
Dash Worcestershire sauce
Salt to taste

In a saucepan, melt butter; blend in next 5 ingredients. Gradually stir in cream; cook and stir till mixture thickens and bubbles. Add remaining ingredients; heat through.

To match picture, pour into individual casseroles; bake in hot oven (400°) for 10 minutes or till top is lightly browned. Serve with Orange Rice and curry condiments: Currant Chutney, finely shredded orange peel, flaked coconut, and chopped roasted peanuts. Makes 4 servings.

Like a citrus cloud, light and fluffy Chalet Suzanne Orange Whip blends the wonderful flavor of fresh oranges with a gentle spike of lemon.

CURRANT CHUTNEY

½ cup chutney, cut in smaller pieces
½ cup red currant jelly
3 tablespoons dried currants
2 tablespoons cooking sherry

Combine ingredients; mix well. Serve with Curry of Shrimp, Suzanne.

Pink shrimp sauced in delicately seasoned cream combine to make Curry of Shrimp, Suzanne superb! Orange Rice, Currant Chutney, and condiments complete the picture.

FLORIDA ORANGE PUNCH

2 cups double-strength, freshly brewed tea
1½ cups sugar
4 cups orange juice
2½ cups unsweetened grapefruit juice
Aromatic bitters

To hot tea, add sugar; stir till dissolved; cool. Add fruit juices. Dash in bitters to taste. Chill. Pour over ice. Garnish with orange slices. Makes about 2 quarts.

Handsomely arranged salad plates are served on the Terrace where you can whiff the ocean breeze and watch the breakers roll in. At left is Americana De Luxe Chicken Salad with triangles of white meat. In center, popular Florida Crab-Stuffed Alligator Pear and at right, refreshing Jumbo Key West Shrimp Plate.

The fresh tang of tree-ripened Florida limes flavors the airy chiffon filling of Americana Key Lime Pie. Topper is a blanket of whipped cream decorated with lime wedges to mark the individual servings.

americana

MIAMI BEACH

Americana

Magnificent describes the Americana; vacationers and conventioners alike speak of it in glowing terms. Every one of its 750 guest rooms offers a view of the Atlantic or of Biscayne Bay, and hospitable friendliness prevails in everything from poolside barbecues to dinner dancing in the formal dining rooms.

This palatial hotel has an enviable reputation for its cuisine. Sixty top-flight chefs have a single purpose: to make each food a work of art, each bite the ultimate in superb eating. There are 4 separate kitchens, one for room service alone. The dining rooms include the Gaucho Steak House where rotisseries and charcoal pits sizzle meat to its palatable best, the Dominion Coffee House, and the elegant Medallion Room used for special buffets and banquets. Now, from these rooms, we bring some of the Americana's favorite and best recipes.

AMERICANA DE LUXE CHICKEN SALAD

Simmer chicken whole, till tender. After thorough chilling, remove wishbone section and breast as one piece; remove bones. Now slice white meat with sharp knife—slices will be triangular. On chilled plates, line chicken slices atop diced celery. Complete salad plate with tomato slices, wedges of hard-cooked egg, green and ripe olives, pickle slices. Garnish with water cress and pimiento slices. Serve with mayonnaise.

JUMBO KEY WEST SHRIMP PLATE

Center each chilled plate with a tower of chilled pink shrimp atop a base of diced celery. (Be careful not to overcook shrimp—about 5 minutes of simmering in water with salt and spices is enough.)

To serve, circle the tower of shrimp with slices of tomato and hard-cooked egg. Add a mound of coleslaw, then tuck in olives, pickle slices, and big juicy wedges of lemon. Offer a tangy cocktail sauce.

One look at this Catullian array of desserts and all thoughts of calorie-counting are gone. The delicate perfection of Americana Rice Pudding (2) rates high with guests. Pineapple Cheesecake (5) is a luscious, delicacy, and Marshmallow Mints Cake (10) wears a candy crown.

1. Strawberry Torte Meringue
2. Americana Rice Pudding*
3. Moka Layer Cake
4. Strawberry Cheesecake
5. Pineapple Cheesecake*
6. Birthday Cake
7. Chocolate Delight
8. Apricot Black-cherry Tartelettes
9. Fancy Fruits Massepain
10. Marshmallow Mints Cake*

*Recipes are given

FLORIDA CRAB-STUFFED ALLIGATOR PEAR

¼ cup mayonnaise
1 tablespoon chopped chives
1½ tablespoons lemon juice
Dash salt and pepper
Dash Worcestershire sauce
1 6½-ounce can (1 cup) crab meat
2 ripe avocados, chilled

Combine first 6 ingredients. Break crab meat in chunks; add to dressing and mix lightly. Chill. Halve avocados lengthwise; remove pits carefully. Pare avocado halves; brush with lemon or grapefruit juice to retain color. To serve, fill avocado halves with the crab-meat salad. Sprinkle with finely chopped hard-cooked eggs. Top with dab of mayonnaise and a spiral of thin ripe-olive wedges centered with a pimiento. Pass Thousand Island dressing. Serves 4.

AMERICANA KEY LIME PIE

1 tablespoon unflavored gelatin
½ cup sugar
¼ teaspoon salt
4 eggs, separated
½ cup lime juice
¼ cup water
1 teaspoon grated lime peel
Few drops green food coloring
½ cup sugar
1 cup whipping cream, whipped
1 baked 9-inch pastry shell

Combine gelatin, ½ cup sugar, and salt. Beat egg *yolks*, lime juice, and water; stir into gelatin. Cook and stir over medium heat just till mixture comes to boiling. Remove from heat; add lime peel. Add coloring to give pale green color. Chill, stirring occasionally, till mixture mounds slightly when dropped from spoon. Beat egg whites to soft peaks; gradually add ½ cup sugar; beat to stiff peaks. Fold gelatin mixture into egg whites. Fold in whipped cream. Pile into cooled baked pastry shell. Chill firm. Spread with additional whipped cream; edge with grated lime peel; center with grated pistachio nuts. Garnish with lime wedges.

AMERICANA RICE PUDDING

4 cups milk, scalded
1 orange peel
½ cup long-grain rice
½ cup sugar
¾ teaspoon salt
. . .
1 cup light cream
2 egg yolks
. . .
½ teaspoon vanilla
. . .
Cinnamon-sugar mixture
Whipped cream
Glaceed or maraschino cherries

Scald milk in top of double boiler over *hot, not boiling*, water. Pare orange like an apple, going round and round so peel is in one long spiral, (use peel only).

To scalded milk add the orange peel, rice, sugar, and salt. Cook covered in top of double boiler over *hot, not boiling*, water until rice is tender, about 45 minutes. Stir occasionally during first part of cooking. Remove orange peel.

Combine cream and egg yolks; stir a small amount of hot mixture into egg yolks; return to hot mixture and mix. Continue cooking covered until mixture thickens, about 20 minutes, stirring now and then. Add vanilla. Pour pudding into custard cups and let cool; chill, if desired.

To serve, sprinkle tops with cinnamon-sugar mixture (1 part sugar and 1 part cinnamon). Garnish with dollups of whipped cream and cherries. Makes 8 servings.

MARSHMALLOW MINTS CAKE

Bake a yellow sponge or chiffon cake in two 8- or 9-inch layers—use a cake mix or your favorite recipe. (Actually, at the Americana they use 3 layers.)

Fill between the layers with mint jelly, then with part of the Marshmallow Frosting. Mask sides of layers with more Marshmallow Frosting and sprinkle generously with chocolate decorettes. Top cake with remaining Marshmallow Frosting and decorate with rows of multicolored candy mints.

MARSHMALLOW FROSTING

1 8-ounce jar marshmallow creme
2 egg whites
1 teaspoon vanilla

Beat together marshmallow creme and unbeaten egg whites on high speed on mixer till fluffy, scraping sides of bowl often. Add vanilla. Makes 3 cups frosting.

PINEAPPLE CHEESECAKE

1½ cups graham-cracker crumbs
. . .
3 pounds cream cheese
2¾ cups sugar
5 tablespoons cornstarch
¼ teaspoon salt
6 eggs
6 egg yolks
¾ cup light cream
Grated peel of 1 lemon
Juice of 1 lemon
¼ teaspoon vanilla
. . .
Canned pineapple rings
Maraschino cherries
Apricot jam

Reserve ½ *cup* of the crumbs. Press remaining crumbs onto bottom and 2 inches up the sides of *generously* buttered 10-inch spring-form pan. Stir cream cheese to soften; beat till fluffy. Mix sugar, cornstarch, and salt; gradually blend into cheese. Add eggs and yolks, one at a time, beating well after each—be sure there are no lumps. Stir in remaining ingredients for filling. Pour into the crumb-lined pan.

Bake in slow oven (325°) for 1 hour and 40 minutes or till done, (cake will not be completely set in center and will have slight depression on top). Cool in pan about 2 hours. Remove sides of pan and arrange pineapple rings and maraschino cherries on top of cake. Glaze by spreading with sieved apricot jam. Sprinkle sides with reserved crumbs. Chill. Makes 20 to 24 servings.

Note: For smaller cheesecake, use ½ recipe; bake in 7-inch spring-form pan at 325° for 1 hour and 20 minutes or till done.

RESTAURANT Fondee en 1840 ANTOINE

NEW ORLEANS

Antoine's

None can deny that Antoine's helped create and maintain New Orleans' matchless reputation for fine food. Antoine Alciatore's grandson, an unsurpassed restaurateur, holds strictly to the excellence established by Grandpere in 1840. Cues waiting in line for tables, can enjoy the fabled St. Louis Street surroundings—some of the oldest and most historic architecture in the French Quarter.

OMELETTE ESPAGNOLE

1 1-pound can (2 cups) tomatoes
1 tablespoon butter or margarine
1 teaspoon salt
Dash *each* black pepper and cayenne
1 tablespoon snipped parsley
¼ teaspoon thyme
1 bay leaf
2 cloves garlic, minced
1 tablespoon butter or margarine
1 tablespoon all-purpose flour
½ cup minced onion
¼ cup chopped green pepper
½ cup white wine
1 3-ounce can sliced mushrooms
½ cup cooked peas
8 eggs
2 tablespoons butter or margarine
2 tablespoons olive oil

Combine first 9 ingredients; cook and stir until mixture is thick, about 30 minutes. Melt 1 tablespoon butter and blend in flour; cook and stir until mixture is browned and thickened. Add onion and green pepper; cook till slightly browned. Add wine; stir till mixture begins to thicken. Add mushrooms, peas, and tomato mixture. Mix well.

Beat 4 eggs well. Add ⅓ *cup* of the hot tomato mixture to the eggs. Heat 1 *tablespoon* butter and 1 *tablespoon* olive oil in a skillet; pour in egg-tomato mixture. Shake skillet till mixture begins to set, lifting edges of omelet to allow uncooked egg to flow under. When cooked fold omelet; pour 1 cup tomato sauce over top.

Repeat using remaining 4 eggs, beaten well and mixed with ⅓ *cup* hot tomato sauce. Heat remaining butter and oil; cook as above. Pour sauce over. Makes 2.

NEW ORLEANS

Arnaud's

Arnaud's most famous name in a city of famous names, is as popular with New Orleanian diners as with travelers. The food is dependably authentic, the menu is the Quarter's longest. Wise men order the specialty of the house and the season, counting on rich Creole heritage from founder Arnaud Cazenave. Mrs. Germaine Wells, upholds her father's venerable philosophy of fine food and service.

FILLET OF RED FISH WITH HOLLANDAISE SAUCE

3 pounds fillet of red snapper
Water to cover*
2 egg yolks
¼ teaspoon dry mustard
1 tablespoon tarragon vinegar
½ cup butter or margarine, melted

Place fish in boiling water; poach until fish flakes. Season to taste. Drain fish and place on warm platter. Keep warm.

For sauce combine egg yolks, mustard, and vinegar; beat well. Continue beating and gradually add butter. Cook and stir over medium heat till sauce thickens. Spoon over fish; dash with paprika. Serves 4.

*To measure water, place fish in pan; pour water over. Remove fish till water boils.

PINEAPPLE AND LOUISIANA YAMS FLAMBEE A LA GERMAINE

Cook, peel, and halve 6 yams. Roll yams and 6 pineapple slices in ⅔ cup all-purpose flour. Then dip in ⅓ cup milk and roll again in flour. In a frying pan melt ½ cup butter or margarine. Brown the coated yams and pineapple in the butter or margarine.

For each serving place 2 yam halves, cut side up, side by side, on an oven-going platter. Top each serving with a browned pineapple slice. Place a maraschino cherry in the center of each pineapple slice. Sprinkle ½ cup brown sugar over all.

Bake in a hot oven (400°) for 5 minutes. Remove from oven. Heat ½ cup rum and pour over hot yams; set aflame. When flame burns out pour 1 teaspoon sherry over each serving. Serve hot. Makes 6 servings.

NEW ORLEANS

Pontchartrain

The Pontchartrain Hotel has developed and preserved an art of gracious service that combines traditions of France and the American South. Situated on St. Charles Avenue in an area between beloved Bourbon Street and the stately Garden District, the Pontchartrain has earned the respect of New Orleans residents not only for its fine hotel service, but for the delicious food it serves. Creole dishes are at their best here, and when fish and sea food of local waters are served, they might well have been prepared in a French kitchen.

Eyes widen when the Pontchartrain's dessert creation comes into view—golden-brown meringue mounded high over layers of ice cream. Shown here on the outdoor garden-patio, Mile High Ice Cream Pie is as large in flavor as it it in size.

HEART OF ARTICHOKE VERSAILLES

3 large artichokes
3 to 4 lemon slices
3 tomato slices, ½-inch thick
½ cup French dressing

• • •

6 hard-cooked eggs, chopped
⅓ cup mayonnaise
½ teaspoon salt
Dash pepper
3 teaspoons caviar
Thousand Island dressing

Wash artichokes. Cut off 1 inch of tops, stems, and tips of leaves. Pull off any loose leaves. Place artichokes and lemon slices in a small amount of boiling salted water; cover. Simmer till a leaf pulls out easily, 25 to 30 minutes. Drain; remove leaves and choke. Chill tomato slices and artichoke bottoms in French dressing for at least 1 hour. Combine eggs, mayonnaise, salt, and pepper; chill. To serve, place a tomato slice in a lettuce cup. Top with an artichoke bottom; pyramid egg salad over both. Top with a teaspoon of caviar. Pass Thousand Island dressing. Makes 3 servings.

MILE HIGH ICE CREAM PIE

1½ cups sifted all-purpose flour
½ teaspoon salt
½ cup shortening
4 to 5 tablespoons cold water
1 pint vanilla ice cream
1 pint chocolate ice cream
4 egg whites
½ teaspoon vanilla
¼ teaspoon cream of tartar
½ cup sugar

Sift together flour and salt. Cut in shortening till pieces are about the size of small peas. Sprinkle 1 tablespoon cold water over flour mixture; gently toss with fork. Repeat till all is moistened. With fingers form into a ball. On lightly floured surface, roll to ⅛ inch thickness. Transfer to a 9-inch pie plate. Fit loosely onto bottom and sides; prick well. Bake in a very hot oven (450°) for 10 to 12 minutes. Cool before filling.

Layer vanilla ice cream in pie shell; then chocolate ice cream. Beat egg whites with vanilla and cream of tartar till soft peaks form. Gradually add sugar, beating till stiff and glossy and sugar is dissolved. Spread meringue over ice cream, sealing to edges of pastry. Broil 30 seconds to 1 minute to brown meringue. Freeze pie several hours or overnight. To serve, slice in wedges and drizzle Chocolate Sauce over each serving. (Or use caramel or Melba sauce).

CHOCOLATE SAUCE

4 1-ounce squares unsweetened chocolate
¾ cup water
1 cup sugar
Dash salt
6 tablespoons butter or margarine
1 teaspoon vanilla

In a saucepan, heat chocolate and water together over low heat, stirring constantly till chocolate is smooth and melted. Add sugar and salt. Simmer till slightly thickened, about 5 minutes. Remove chocolate mixture from heat, blend in butter and vanilla. Serve warm over Mile High Ice Cream Pie. Makes about 1¾ cups sauce.

SHRIMP SAKI

1 pound jumbo shrimp, cleaned and peeled
Dash salt
Dash pepper
Dash paprika
2 tablespoons lemon juice
⅓ cup butter or margarine, melted

Split shrimp from back and wash thoroughly under running water; place on a baking sheet. Season with salt and pepper; sprinkle with paprika. Bake in a hot oven (425°) for 8 minutes. Remove from oven and place under broiler for 5 minutes. Combine lemon juice and melted butter; serve with shrimp. Makes 4 to 6 servings.

DEVILED OYSTERS ON THE HALF SHELL

14 oysters in shell
2 tablespoons finely chopped shallots
1 tablespoon butter or margarine
2 tablespoons all-purpose flour
½ teaspoon salt
⅛ teaspoon nutmeg
Dash cayenne
1 tablespoon Worcestershire sauce
½ teaspoon chopped parsley
½ teaspoon prepared mustard
1 3-ounce can chopped mushrooms, drained
1 slightly beaten egg yolk
½ cup cracker crumbs
1 tablespoon butter or margarine, melted

Open oysters and reserve ⅓ cup of the liquor. With a knife, remove oysters from shells; wash thoroughly and chop. Wash shells. Cook shallots in 1 tablespoon butter till just tender; blend in flour and let brown. Stir in reserved oyster liquor, salt, nutmeg, cayenne, Worcestershire, parsley, mustard, and mushrooms; add oysters. Cook about 3 minutes, stirring constantly. Remove from heat and add egg yolk. Spoon mixture into deep halves of oyster shells. Combine cracker crumbs and melted butter; sprinkle over oyster mixture. Bake in a moderate oven (350°) for about 10 minutes. Serve immediately. Makes 2 to 3 servings.

NEW ORLEANS

Commander's Palace

People may eat fine foods throughout the United States, but in New Orleans as perhaps nowhere else, there is opportunity for real dining. Commander's Palace at the corner of Washington Avenue and Coliseum Street consistently presents the quality that has made it a favorite social gathering place for residents of New Orleans. Located in the artistocratic Garden District, the dining garden of Commander's Palace is one of the loveliest to be found in the city. Owner Frank Moran and his wife Elinor act as host and hostess, and if you're in the mood to experiment and especially if you are a newcomer to New Orleans, your waiter or the Maitre d'Hotel knows how to do a superb job of selecting foods.

SHRIMP A L'IMPERATRICE

1 cup mayonnaise
1 teaspoon dry mustard
3 tablespoons chopped pimiento
¼ cup finely diced green pepper
½ teaspoon salt
2 cups cleaned cooked shrimp (1½ pounds in shell), *or* 2 4½-ounce cans shrimp
3 avocados, peeled and halved
2 teaspoons fine dry bread crumbs
Paprika

Thoroughly combine mayonnaise and mustard. Add chopped pimiento, green pepper, and salt; mix well. Fold in cleaned shrimp. Fill each avocado half, cut side up, with shrimp mixture (you may have to slice off bottom of avocados to get them to stand upright). Sprinkle tops with bread crumbs and paprika. Serve hot or cold. To serve hot, bake at 350° for 10 to 15 minutes or till heated through. To serve cold, chill shrimp mixture before filling avocado halves. Pass lemon wedges. Makes 6 servings.

BANANAS FOSTER

6 large all-yellow bananas
Lemon juice

• • •

1 cup brown sugar
½ cup butter or margarine

• • •

Cinnamon

Peel the bananas and halve lengthwise, then brush with lemon juice. Melt brown sugar and butter in flat chafing dish. Add bananas; cook just until tender. Sprinkle with cinnamon. Serve as is or with vanilla ice cream. Makes 6 servings.

EGGS HUSSARDE

Lay slices of grilled Canadian bacon on crisp rusks; cover with Marchand de Vin Sauce. Top with grilled tomato slices, then Soft-poached Eggs. Ladle Hollandaise Sauce over; garnish with a sprinkling of paprika.

MARCHAND DE VIN SAUCE

½ cup butter or margarine
⅓ cup finely chopped mushrooms
½ cup minced ham
⅓ cup finely chopped shallots or green onions
½ cup finely chopped onion
2 or 3 cloves garlic, minced

• • •

2 tablespoons flour
⅛ teaspoon pepper
Dash cayenne

• • •

¾ cup beef stock (*or* use ½ cup canned condensed beef broth and ¼ cup water)
½ cup cooking claret

In a 9-inch skillet melt butter and lightly saute the mushrooms, ham, shallots, onion, and garlic. When the onion is tender, add the flour, pepper, and cayenne. Brown mixture nicely, about 7 to 10 minutes, stirring constantly. Blend in the beef stock and the claret wine. Cover and simmer over low heat for about 15 minutes, stirring occasionally. Makes about 1½ cups sauce.

NEW ORLEANS

Brennan's

If you want the best in Creole-French cuisine served in one of New Orleans' most lovely historic mansions, visit Brennan's. Manager Ella Brennan Martin took over direction of the Brennan restaurant kitchen when she was just 18. She studied old French and Southern cook books, and with the help of Head Chef Paul Blange, developed recipes for the most popular dishes of old New Orleans. The Brennan success story is based on a challenge first accepted by the late founder (Ella's brother)—and now by all the Brennan clan: To show the world that a French-Quarter Irish family can run a Creole restaurant second to none!

The dinner and luncheon menu offer wide variety, but breakfast at Brennan's is the specialty and may be ordered any time of day—from 9:00 a.m. to midnight! Sunday morning is the most popular time for a breakfast that may last several hours. In the Brennan kitchen there's a fast tempo, but guests enjoy the leisurely "fork breakfast" (*dejeuner a la fourchette*) with all the gracious Southern hospitality of plantation days. Even the menu entreats diners not to hurry—and some patrons have been known to come in the morning and stay on for an evening meal in the soft glow of candles and crystal chandeliers.

A "typical New Orleans breakfast" starts with grilled grapefruit, continues with Eggs Hussarde, and builds up to a grand finale of Bananas Foster (at left) prepared in a chafing dish at the table. Other Brennan specialties include Eggs Benedict (pictured on next page); Shrimp Etouffe (*say ay-too-fay*), a creole recipe for shrimp in a deliciously spiced tomato puree; Spanish Rice with a touch of saffron for distinctive flavor and color; and Hors d'oeuvre Crab Ravigotte, an appetizer salad spiked with horseradish and mustard. For dessert, spoon Praline Parfait Sauce over vanilla ice cream to make luscious Southern sundaes.

HOLLANDAISE SAUCE

4 egg yolks
1 to 2 tablespoons lemon juice
• • •
½ pound (2 sticks or 1 cup) butter or margarine, melted
¼ teaspoon salt

In top of double boiler, beat egg yolks slightly and stir in lemon juice. Place over *hot, not boiling* water—don't allow water in bottom pan to touch top pan. Add butter a little at a time, stirring constantly with wooden spoon. Add the salt, and pepper to taste. Continue cooking slowly just until mixture thickens—stirring all the time. Makes 1 cup.

EGGS BENEDICT

Top crisp rusks with round slices of grilled Canadian-style bacon and hot Soft-poached Eggs. Ladle tangy Hollandaise Sauce over the eggs and sprinkle with paprika. Garnish with truffle slices and sprigs of parsley. Serve immediately.

SOFT-POACHED EGGS

In a large saucepan, heat water (about an octave deep) to boiling. Add a little vinegar and salt to the boiling water.

Break each egg into saucedish, then slide egg into the water, tipping dish toward edge of pan. Keep heat low—don't let water boil. When soft cooked, about 3 to 5 minutes, remove eggs with slotted spoon or pancake turner. To keep them hot until ready to serve, transfer the poached eggs to warm water (about 3 inches deep).

CHICKEN MARCHAND DE VIN

Choose a 2½- to 3-pound ready-to-cook broiler-fryer chicken, disjointed. Dredge chicken pieces in seasoned flour and fry until tender, covering when golden brown. Transfer chicken to baking dish; pour Marchand de Vin Sauce over. Bake uncovered in moderate oven (350°) for about 15 to 20 minutes. Makes 3 or 4 servings.

HOR D'OEUVRE CRAB RAVIGOTTE

½ cup mayonnaise
1 tablespoon *each* minced parsley, and drained capers, finely chopped
1½ teaspoons dry mustard
1½ teaspoons prepared horseradish
1 tablespoon chopped pimiento
1 hard-cooked egg, finely chopped
¼ teaspoon lemon juice
1 cup lump crab meat

Combine first 8 ingredients. Add crab meat; toss lightly; chill. Serve in individual shells. Garnish with pimiento strips and tomato half-slices. Makes 4 servings.

SHRIMP ETOUFFE

1 medium onion, finely chopped
2 finely chopped green onions
3 or 4 cloves garlic, minced
¼ cup finely chopped celery
½ cup butter or margarine
2 tablespoons flour
2½ cups water
1 10½-ounce can (1¼ cups) tomato puree
2 bay leaves
1 tablespoon Worcestershire sauce
4 drops bottled hot pepper sauce
1 teaspoon salt
½ teaspoon sugar
½ teaspoon whole thyme, crushed
⅛ teaspoon pepper
1 pound (3 cups) cleaned raw shrimp (2 pounds in shell)
2 hard-cooked eggs, quartered

Saute first 4 ingredients in butter till tender. Add flour; cook and stir till lightly browned. Add next 9 ingredients; simmer uncovered, stirring occasionally, 25 minutes, or till almost desired consistency. Add shrimp; cook 15 minutes more. Garnish with eggs. Serve with rice. Serves 4 to 6.

Eggs Benedict is an elegant stack-up of crispy rusks, grilled rounds of Canadian bacon, perfect poached eggs, and a generous ladle of rich, tangy Hollandaise Sauce. Truffle trim adds final touch. →

HAMBURGER STEAK, BRENNAN

2 pounds ground beef
¼ cup minced shallots or green onions
¼ cup minced white onion
½ cup toasted fine rusk crumbs
1 teaspoon salt
½ teaspoon pepper
Dash nutmeg
2 tablespoons Worcestershire sauce
1 tablespoon chopped parsley
1 egg

Combine ingredients; mix well. Shape into 6 oval patties. Grill to preferred doneness. Serve with Sauce Maison.

SAUCE MAISON

¼ pound (½ cup) butter or margarine
1 tablespoon Worcestershire sauce
¾ cup *glace de viande* (from beef), *or* use canned condensed beef broth
Pinch chopped parsley

Melt butter, heating till golden brown. Add Worcestershire and *glace de viande;* cook 1 minute. Add parsley. Serve hot.

SPANISH RICE

½ cup chopped green pepper
¾ cup chopped white onion
⅓ cup chopped ham
½ teaspoon Spanish saffron, crushed
⅓ cup butter or margarine
3 cups cooked rice
½ teaspoon white pepper
⅓ cup chopped pimiento
1 tablespoon liquid from pimiento

Saute first 4 ingredients in butter over medium heat till vegetables are tender. Stir in remaining ingredients; heat through. Salt to taste. Makes 4 to 6 servings.

PRALINE PARFAIT SAUCE

2 cups dark corn syrup
⅓ cup sugar
⅓ cup boiling water
1 cup chopped pecans, toasted

In saucepan, combine syrup, sugar, and water. Cook and stir over medium heat just till mixture comes to boiling; remove from heat. Cool. Add pecans. Makes 2½ cups.

Neiman-Marcus

DALLAS

Neiman-Marcus

"Very Neiman-Marcus" applies to the quality merchandise of this world-famous specialty store—to its beautiful fashion models—to its discriminating and chic customers—and just as much to the food artistry of its Zodiac Room.

Stanley Marcus, president, and two of his brothers have a busy hand in the specialty store, but they confidently leave the whole domain of the Zodiac Room (and the employees' Little Dipper) to Home Economist-Dietitian Helen Corbitt. This dramatic, night-blue dining room and terrace with its decorative signs of the zodiac is a popular rendezvous all day. Always for lunch and afternoon tea—for dinner on Thursday evenings (the store is open that night)—for teen-age parties and civic-benefit dinners. The big event of the year is the Neiman-Marcus Fashion Exposition where many world-renowned *couturiers* vie for "Oscars."

To read Zodiac menus is appetite provoking—and fun. Children may select from their own *carte du jour*. While you make your selection, a demitasse cup of tasty soup is served, courtesy of Neiman-Marcus. At the buffet table (left), guests help themselves to Ham Rolls, Rock Cornish Hen, Roquefort-stuffed Shrimp, and Seven-layer Cake with Chocolate Butter Frosting.

HAM ROLLS

Spread thin ham slices sparingly with butter and finely chopped chutney. Roll up each ham slice, beginning with narrow side. Chill several hours or overnight. Slice rolls diagonally for attractive service.

ROCK CORNISH HENS

Sprinkle tiny Rock Cornish Hens with salt and pepper; roast, breast down. When tender, turn them over and baste with mixture of honey and butter in equal proportions. Perch preserved kumquats on drumsticks.

ROQUEFORT-STUFFED SHRIMP

2 dozen large fresh or frozen shrimp

• • •

1 3-ounce package cream cheese
1 ounce Roquefort or blue cheese, crumbled
½ teaspoon prepared mustard
Dash garlic salt

• • •

1 cup finely chopped parsley

Place shrimp in boiling salted water to cover. Cover pan; bring to boiling, then lower heat and simmer gently till shrimp turn pink, about 5 minutes. Drain and peel. Split each shrimp part way down along vein side; remove vein and clean. Chill. Blend remaining ingredients except parsley; chill. Using a pastry tube, stuff shrimp with chilled cheese mixture. Roll cheese side in parsley.

BABY CROOKNECK SQUASH

Select yellow summer squashes, less than 3 inches long. Steam till tender. Split lengthwise; brush cut surface generously with melted butter. Season with salt and pepper. Sprinkle liberally with chopped parsley and chopped pimiento. Place in shallow pan; heat in moderate oven just till they sizzle.

CELERY ORIENTAL

Cut 6 to 8 large, outside celery stalks diagonally. Cook in a little boiling salted water until just crisp-done, (you have to taste); drain. Saute 1 cup sliced fresh mushrooms in 3 tablespoons butter; add the celery and ¼ cup toasted almond halves. Toss around lightly till heated. Makes 4 to 6 servings.

ASPARAGUS WITH CROUTONS

Dice bread—white, whole wheat, or rye—in ⅛-inch squares. Brown in a little butter in skillet or fry in deep hot fat. Season with salt and pepper, garlic salt, curry powder, or any favorite herb. Sprinkle over hot buttered asparagus. (Or, try with green beans, broccoli, or cauliflower.)

SEVEN-LAYER CAKE

¾ cup shortening
3⅓ cups sifted cake flour
2¼ cups sugar
4½ teaspoons baking powder
1½ teaspoons salt

• • •

1½ cups milk
3 eggs
2 teaspoons vanilla

Stir shortening just to soften. Sift in dry ingredients. Add *1 cup of the milk;* mix until all flour is dampened. Then beat vigorously 2 minutes. Add remaining milk, eggs, and vanilla. Beat vigorously 2 minutes longer. Pour about *2 cups* batter into a lightly greased and floured 9x1½-inch round pan. Tip pan so batter runs over bottom. Invert pan over baking sheet and tap edges on baking sheet, allowing as much batter to run out of pan as will do so easily. Turn pan right side up, scrape down sides to prevent burning, and even out batter remaining on bottom. Repeat for other 6 layers, baking as many at a time as you have pans and oven space.* Bake in hot oven (400°) 8 minutes or till done. Cool in pans 3 to 5 minutes, then invert on rack to cool. Put layers together and frost with Chocolate Butter Frosting.

*While baking first layers, keep remaining cake batter in refrigerator.

CHOCOLATE BUTTER FROSTING (FOR SEVEN-LAYER CAKE)

3 cups sifted confectioners' sugar
⅓ cup hot water
4 1-ounce squares unsweetened chocolate, melted
1 slightly beaten egg
½ cup soft butter or margarine
1½ teaspoons vanilla

Blend sugar and hot water into melted chocolate. With spoon beat half of egg into chocolate mixture; beat in remaining egg. Beat in butter, a tablespoon at a time. Blend in vanilla. Frosting will be thin at this point, so place bowl in pan of ice water and beat till of spreading consistency.

RICH COOKIES

½ cup butter or margarine
⅓ cup sugar
1 well-beaten egg
¾ cup sifted all-purpose flour
½ teaspoon vanilla
Raisins, blanched almonds or citron

Cream butter; add sugar gradually, creaming well. Stir in egg, then flour and vanilla. Drop from tip of teaspoon on ungreased baking sheet; spread thinly with knife first dipped in cold water. Center each with raisin, slivered almond, or small piece of citron. Bake at 375° for 7 or 8 minutes. Remove immediately to rack. Makes 5 dozen.

PECAN DAINTIES

1 egg white
Dash salt
1 cup light brown sugar
1½ cups pecan halves

Beat egg white with salt to soft peaks. Add brown sugar in 2 additions; beat lightly after each. (Mixture will be thin.) Stir in nuts; drop, 2 inches apart, from a teaspoon onto greased baking sheet. Bake at 250° about 30 minutes. Remove from baking sheet immediately. Makes about 3½ dozen.

OPEN-FACE APPLE PIE

1 10-inch unbaked pie shell
11 cups quartered pared tart apples
2 cups sugar
4 tablespoons all-purpose flour
1 teaspoon salt
⅓ cup light cream
¼ cup milk
⅛ teaspoon cinnamon

Fill pie shell with the quartered apples. Thoroughly combine sugar, flour, and salt; add cream and milk; beat. Cover apples with mixture. Sprinkle with cinnamon. Bake at 375° for 1½ to 2 hours or till apples are soft. (Cover pie loosely with foil for first hour of baking, then remove foil.) Serve warm with scoops of aged Cheddar.

These teatime tidbits are passed to everyone regardless of what they may order. The top deck includes paper-thin Rich Cookies, and Pecan Dainties. Below, Bachelors-buttons are favored by men.

BACHELORS-BUTTONS

¾ cup butter or margarine
1 cup brown sugar
1 egg
2 cups sifted all-purpose flour
1 teaspoon soda
¼ teaspoon salt
¼ teaspoon ginger
¼ teaspoon cinnamon
1 teaspoon vanilla
1 cup chopped nuts
Sugar

Cream butter; add the brown sugar gradually and beat well. Add unbeaten egg. Sift together flour, soda, salt, ginger, and cinnamon; stir dry mixture into butter mixture. Fold in vanilla and chopped nuts. Chill dough for several hours. Make into small balls (1 level teaspoon dough for tiny cookies, 2 for medium). Dip balls into granulated sugar; place 2 inches apart on lightly buttered baking sheet, and press down with the tines of a fork. Bake in a moderate oven (375°) about 8 to 10 minutes, or until nicely browned. Makes 12 dozen small cookies.

HOUSTON

Maxim's

With surprising success, Camille Bermann, proprietor of Maxim's, has introduced many a wary Texan to the gustatory delights of continental Europe. A native of Luxembourg, Mr. Bermann is now a resident of Houston. His restaurant expertly presents the highly developed cuisine of Old World countries to a growing and changing Western American area. The food Mr. Bermann serves is an example of the best in continental cookery. Fish and poultry dishes abound on the menu, many of them sauced with the delicate blend of flavors only an expert can achieve. Imported wines are served in oversized crystal glasses, and the desserts offered are masterpieces of French cookery. Chocolat Mousse with just a hint of mocha flavor is listed on the menu among delicate pastries, ice creams, filled crepes, and fruits flamed in liqueurs.

But Texas has wielded its influence too. Thick tender steaks and prime ribs are available cooked to order, and service comes from a staff of well-trained and attractive waitresses—an American touch that most customers seem to like.

CHOCOLAT MOUSSE

4 1-ounce squares semisweet chocolate
2 tablespoons water
2 tablespoons instant coffee

. . .

5 egg yolks
5 egg whites
¼ cup sugar
1 cup whipping cream, whipped

Combine chocolate, water, and instant coffee in top of double boiler; stir over *hot, not boiling* water till chocolate melts. Transfer mixture to a mixing bowl; add egg yolks, one at a time, beating well after each. Beat egg whites till soft peaks form; gradually add sugar, beating to stiff peaks. Fold egg whites into chocolate mixture. Then fold in whipped cream. Spoon into sherbet dishes; chill at least 3 hours before serving. Serves 8.

LOUISVILLE

The Old House Restaurant

The Old House Restaurant was built in the 1830s as a town house for Judge John Rowan, owner of Federal Hill (My Old Kentucky Home). After his death three generations of the Canine family lived and worked as dentists in the Old House. During their residence, "Rosepearl" or celluloid was invented in the house. It was also the Canine family who shocked Louisville with the first electrically lighted home of the area. The first night, neighboring residents were so apprehensive that they called the fire department.

The Old House has retained its ante-bellum appearance among buildings of much more modern form, but behind the southern facade is found one of the finest restaurants sophisticated Louisville can offer. A range of international cuisine includes Dover sole from the English Channel, lobster from the cold waters of Maine, shrimp from the Gulf of Mexico, and escargots from France.

CAFE BRULOT DIABOLIQUE

3 inches stick cinnamon
6 whole cloves
2 sugar cubes
1 teaspoon grated lemon peel
1 teaspoon grated orange peel
¼ cup brandy
2½ cups strong freshly brewed coffee

In a chafing dish or Brulot bowl, combine 3 inches stick cinnamon, whole cloves, sugar cubes, grated lemon and grated orange peel. Add ¼ cup brandy. Heat, stirring mixture frequently, until sugar cubes are melted and brandy is hot. Set mixture aflame. When liquid is flaming high, pour in strong freshly brewed coffee. Serve immediately. Makes about 4 servings.

MEMPHIS

Justine's

Regional dishes of elegant tradition—so says a restaurant guide, but there's so much more at Justine's in Memphis. Dayton and Justine Smith restored a stately old house to bring back its French colonial grandeur. Old Coward Place, it was called and pointed to as a Memphis landmark.

When Justine opened it as a restaurant, (moving from an already well-known restaurant where she was highly respected for talented management and gracious hospitality) first-nighters exclaimed about its new look, which wasn't really new at all. Herringbone walls of handmade bricks from the old mansion, fired in an old kiln discovered on the estate, were rebuilt. Rescued old wrought-iron window guards, patio gates, settees, balustrades, and banisters helped recapture early Memphis styles. The warm soft pink stonecote exterior duplicated the original color, discovered under coat after coat of old paint. Around the mansion, meandering walks curve through green-gardened areas of boxwood, cherry laurel, camellia, and magnolia. Magnificent candelabra light the foyer and steps of a graceful curving stairway. Rooms, 14 feet high, that once dignified settings for belles and beaux at ante-bellum parties, now glow again with beauty and animation and with the anticipation of the finest of foods prepared only upon order. Damask walls, pier mirrors and paintings by fine artists give permanence to the decor. Memphis people praise this authentic restoration, hoping it may stand firm in an area where its once contemporary homes have been leveled by the relentless march of time. The Smiths believe that "he who loves an old house will never love in vain." The food served at Justine's lives up to the elegant surroundings. Shown in the "Cellar Room" are two notable sea food dishes—Crab Meat Suzette and Cassola de Peix.

As Southern as the magnolia branches in the background, scoops of Fresh Garden Mint Ice Cream and almond-flavored Lotus Ice Cream are special spring desserts at Justine's. Fresh strawberries speak for themselves whether served in stemmed glasses or glazed and perched atop cheesecake.

FRESH GARDEN MINT ICE CREAM

1½ cups sugar
1½ cups water
1 cup finely crushed fresh pineapple
2 cups finely crushed fresh mint leaves
1 cup light corn syrup
1 cup canned unsweetened pineapple juice
2 cups milk
2 cups whipping cream
¼ cup creme de menthe

Combine sugar and water; cook and stir till mixture boils. Cook to soft ball stage (236°). Add mint leaves; cook about 10 minutes longer. Remove from heat; strain. Add corn syrup; let cool. Add remaining ingredients; freeze in hand-turned or electric ice cream freezer. Let ripen. Makes 2 quarts.

LOTUS ICE CREAM

2⅔ cups light cream
1 cup sugar
⅓ cup lemon juice
⅓ cup chopped toasted almonds
1½ teaspoons grated lemon rind
½ teaspoon vanilla
⅛ teaspoon almond extract

Combine all ingredients in a mixing bowl stirring till sugar is dissolved. Freeze in a hand-turned or electric ice cream freezer. Makes 1 quart ice cream.

Note: To ripen ice cream, remove ice to below lid of can; take off lid. Remove dasher. Plug opening in lid; cover inside of lid with several thicknesses of waxed paper; replace lid. Pack more ice and salt around can. Cover freezer with heavy cloth or newspapers. Let ripen about 4 hours.

CRAB MEAT SUZETTE

⅓ cup sifted all-purpose flour
1 tablespoon sugar
Dash salt
1 egg
1 egg yolk
¾ cup milk
1 tablespoon butter or margarine, melted

• • •

1 tablespoon butter or margarine
1 tablespoon all-purpose flour
Dash salt
Dash white pepper
½ cup milk
1 cup fresh lump crab meat *or* 1 6-ounce package frozen crab meat
1 tablespoon lemon juice
2 teaspoons sherry
Dash bottled hot pepper sauce
Dash Worcestershire sauce

• • •

½ cup Hollandaise sauce

Measure the first 7 ingredients into a blender container or mixing bowl; blend or beat with an electric or rotary beater till batter is smooth. Refrigerate several hours or till batter is thick.

In a saucepan, melt 1 tablespoon butter over low heat. Blend in flour, salt, and white pepper. Add milk all at once; cook quickly, stirring constantly, till mixture thickens and bubbles. Add crab meat, lemon juice, sherry, hot pepper sauce, and Worcestershire sauce; heat through and keep warm.

Heat a heavy 6-inch skillet till a drop of water will dance on the surface. Grease lightly and pour in 2 tablespoons of the chilled batter. Lift skillet off heat and tilt from side to side till batter covers the bottom of the skillet evenly. Return skillet to heat and cook till underside is lightly browned, about 1½ minutes. Remove crepe by inverting skillet over paper towels. Cook remaining crepes the same way, on one side only. Spread 1 tablespoon of the hot crab meat filling across each crepe. Place in a hot oven (400°) and heat till edges of crepes begin to toast. Remove from oven and spoon Hollandaise sauce over. Serve as appetizer or entree. Makes about 11 crepes.

CASSOLA DE PEIX
(Sea-food Casserole)

2 tablespoons butter or margarine
2 tablespoons all-purpose flour
¼ teaspoon salt
1 cup milk
12 medium shrimp, cooked and split *or* 1 4½-ounce can shrimp
1½ cups fresh lump crab meat *or* 1 7½-ounce can crab meat
1 cup steamed lobster *or* 1 5½-ounce can lobster
1 3-ounce can sliced cooked mushrooms, drained
2 tablespoons sherry
1 tablespoon lemon juice
Dash bottled hot pepper sauce
¼ teaspoon Worcestershire sauce

• • •

½ cup shredded sharp process cheese
1 cup soft bread crumbs
2 tablespoons butter or margarine, melted

Melt butter over low heat. Blend in flour and salt. Add milk all at once. Cook quickly, stirring constantly, till sauce thickens and bubbles; remove from heat. Add next 8 ingredients; mix well. Place mixture in a 1 quart casserole dish. Sprinkle cheese over top. Combine bread crumbs and melted butter; sprinkle over cheese. Bake in a 375° oven for 40 minutes or till heated through. If desired, garnish top with mushroom caps and additional sea food. Serves 4 to 6.

CREME D' EPINARDS
(Creamed Spinach)

1 pound fresh spinach, cooked
¼ cup medium white sauce
½ teaspoon salt
Dash pepper
Dash Worcestershire sauce
Dash bottled hot pepper sauce
¼ cup Hollandaise sauce

Chop and drain spinach; add next 5 ingredients and mix thoroughly. Spread into an 8-inch pie plate and top with Hollandaise sauce. Brown lightly in a hot oven (425°) for 15 minutes. Makes 4 servings.

SHELBYVILLE

Old Stone Inn

The reputation of Southern Hospitality stays alive because of such gracious women as Mrs. Virginia Snider and her sisters Mrs. Elizabeth Plues and Mrs. Amie Nilsson. Since its opening in 1924, the Old Stone Inn at Shelbyville, Kentucky, has known these ladies. The Inn itself has a remarkable history. Built before Civil War days, it is now more than 150 years old. In early Kentucky days, Old Stone Inn was a resting station for stage coaches. Legend records that on one occasion French statesmen and General Lafayette stopped here.

As its name implies, the Inn is made of stone, but no mortar holds these walls together. Their construction is so close-fit that even wind and rain are repelled. Inside, the Inn looks less like a restaurant than a home, and visitors feel less like customers than guests. Within gaily papered walls, beautifully finished Early American tables are covered with whitest linen or lace tablecloths. On each table a bouquet of fresh garden flowers invites pleasant conversation. Huge fireplaces and corner cupboards such as the one pictured at left are touches that add to the comfortable homelike atmosphere of Old Stone Inn.

Food served at Old Stone Inn receives every bit as much attention as that given to decor. Pictured at left are two of the most well-liked of old Southern dishes, Stuffed Eggplant served in its own shell, and piping-hot Corn Fritters. Fine pieces of silver and china that have belonged to Mrs. Snider's family for many years present these foods in a most elegant manner.

Old Stone Inn opens its doors to the public only seven months of the year—April through October. During these months, three seasons of the changing year are beautifully reflected in the surrounding trees and hills of Kentucky.

STUFFED EGGPLANT

1 large eggplant
½ cup water
½ teaspoon salt
• • •
¼ cup chopped onion
1 tablespoon butter or margarine
1 tablespoon chopped parsley
1 10½-ounce can condensed cream of mushroom soup
1 teaspoon Worcestershire sauce
1 cup fine rich round cracker crumbs (about 24 crackers)
1 tablespoon butter or margarine
1½ cups water

Slice off one side of eggplant. Remove pulp to within ½ inch of skin. Heat water and salt to boiling. Cook eggplant pulp in the water till tender, about 10 minutes; drain thoroughly. Cook onion in butter till tender but not brown. Add eggplant pulp, parsley, soup, Worcestershire and all of cracker crumbs *except* 2 tablespoons. Fill eggplant shell with mixture. Place in a 10x6x1½-inch baking dish. Dot with 1 tablespoon butter; sprinkle reserved crumbs over top. Carefully pour 1½ cups water in bottom of dish. Bake in a moderate oven (375°) for 1 hour or till heated through. Serves 4 to 6.

CORN FRITTERS

¾ cup sifted all-purpose flour
2 teaspoons baking powder
1 teaspoon sugar
½ teaspoon salt
1 beaten egg
½ cup milk
2 cups (about 6 ears) cut, fresh corn *or* 1 1-pound can whole kernel corn, drained
Sifted confectioners' sugar

Sift together dry ingredients. Combine beaten egg, milk, and corn; add to dry ingredients. Mix just till flour is moistened. Drop batter by level tablespoons into deep, hot fat (375°). Fry until golden brown, about 3 to 4 minutes. Drain on paper towels. Dust with sifted confectioners' sugar; serve warm. Makes about 1½ dozen fritters.

BAKED STUFFED YELLOW SQUASH

3 small yellow summer squashes
Salt to taste
• • •
¼ pound highly seasoned pork sausage
½ cup chopped onion
¾ cup cooked rice
2 tablespoons chopped parsley
½ teaspoon salt
Dash pepper
• • •
1 1-pound can (2 cups) tomatoes
Dash salt
Dash pepper
1 teaspoon sugar
1 clove garlic, minced
1 3-ounce can (⅔ cup) broiled sliced mushrooms, drained
• • •
⅓ cup rich round cracker crumbs (about 8 crackers)
2 tablespoons butter or margarine, melted

In a saucepan, cook yellow squash in boiling salted water until skin is tender, about 10 minutes. Cut each squash in half; remove seeds and pulp from the center to within ½ inch of the skin. Mash the pulp and seeds together. Sprinkle the shells with salt to taste and set aside.

In a large skillet, brown the sausage; drain off excess fat. Add chopped onion; cook until onion is tender but not brown. Stir in cooked rice, mashed squash, parsley, ½ teaspoon salt, and pepper; spoon mixture into squash shells. Place shells in a 13x9x2-inch baking dish.

In a saucepan, combine canned tomatoes, dash salt and pepper, sugar, and minced garlic. Simmer tomato mixture uncovered for 15 minutes. Add sliced mushrooms and pour over stuffed squash.

Combine cracker crumbs and the 2 tablespoons melted butter. Sprinkle each stuffed shell with about 1 tablespoon of the buttered crumb mixture. Bake in a moderate oven (375°) for 30 minutes or until squash is heated through. If desired garnish with sprigs of parsley. Makes 6 servings.

INDIANAPOLIS

L. S. Ayres' Tea Room

The Hoosier shopper drives a hard bargain for quality. L. S. Ayres & Company's Tea Room on the 8th floor of the Ayres' department store meets this demand every day in the food and service it provides. Food creations here are quality pace setters in flavor and appearance. A light touch of the Georgian period hints relaxed elegance to hungry and weary shoppers. For the late shopper who needs a luxury pickup, high tea in candle-lit atmosphere is served each afternoon.

CANADIAN CHEESE SOUP

¼ cup minced onion
2 tablespoons butter or margarine
¼ cup all-purpose flour
2 cups *each* milk and chicken stock
¼ cup finely diced carrot
¼ cup finely diced celery
Dash *each* salt and paprika
½ cup cubed sharp process cheese

Cook onion in butter till tender but not brown. Blend in flour; add next 6 ingredients. Cook and stir till mixture thickens and comes to a boil. Reduce heat and add cheese; stir till cheese melts. Simmer 15 minutes. Makes 4 cups.

CHICKEN VELVET SOUP

6 tablespoons butter or margarine
6 tablespoons all-purpose flour
½ cup milk
½ cup light cream
3 cups chicken broth

• • •

1 cup finely chopped cooked chicken
Dash pepper

Melt butter in saucepan. Blend in flour; add milk, cream, and broth. Cook, stirring constantly, till mixture thickens and comes to a boil; reduce heat. Stir in chicken and pepper. Return to boiling and serve immediately. Makes about 5 cups soup.

CINCINNATI

Maisonette

The Maisonette is an authentically French restaurant, and one of the best in the country. Most of the traditional French dishes are served here, along with just the proper wines which Owner Lee Comisar stocks in his wisely chosen wine cellar. An example of the Maisonette's *haute cuisine* is Filet Mignon Princess (left) which is truly fit for royalty. It's a delectable tower of artichoke, mushroom puree, filet mignon, and asparagus tips, topped with a delicious Bearnaise Sauce.

FILET MIGNON PRINCESS

In skillet, cook 1 tablespoon finely chopped onion in 1 tablespoon butter till tender, but not brown. Mince 2 cups fresh mushrooms; add to onions; cook till liquid is almost gone. Add 2 tablespoons lemon juice and ½ cup red Burgundy wine; reduce to half. Remove from heat. Slightly beat 1 egg yolk; add small amount hot mixture to egg yolk; return to hot mixture; cook and stir till thickened. Fill 4 artichoke cups* with mushroom mixture; keep hot. In another skillet, melt 1 tablespoon shortening; season 4 8-ounce center-cut filet mignons with salt and pepper; pan broil 20 minutes, or to desired doneness. Remove from heat; place on stuffed artichoke cups. Pour excess fat from skillet; add ½ cup red Burgundy wine to pan; reduce to half; pour over meat. Place 3 cooked asparagus tips on each steak; top each with 1 tablespoon Bearnaise. Serve with hot chateau potatoes. Serves 4.

Bearnaise Sauce: In small saucepan, combine 3 tablespoons tarragon vinegar, 1 teaspoon minced shallots, 4 crushed peppercorns, and a bouquet of a few tarragon and chervil leaves; simmer till liquid is reduced to half. Strain; add 1 tablespoon cold water to herb liquid. Beat 4 egg yolks in top of double boiler (not over heat); slowly add herb liquid. Have ½ cup butter at room temperature. Add a *few tablespoons* of the butter to egg yolks; place over *hot, not boiling,* water. Cook and stir till butter melts and sauce starts to thicken. Continue adding butter and stirring till all has been used and sauce is smooth as thick cream. Remove from heat at once. Salt to taste and add 1 teaspoon minced fresh tarragon. (Or, add ¼ teaspoon dried whole tarragon and strain sauce.) Makes about 1 cup.

*Available in cans. (These are artichoke bottoms, or *fonds*, 2 inches in diameter.)

The Tavern

CLEVELAND

The Tavern Chop House

The Tavern Chop House in Cleveland, Ohio boasts a very masculine atmosphere and a very feminine owner-manager. Gracious and competent Mrs. Marie Schreiber knows from her career in quality food service exactly what to feature on her menu to please anxious appetites.

In the picture, Mrs. Schreiber is arranging thin slices of Roast Canadian Bacon. This specialty of the house has a luscious pineapple glaze, is accompanied by a mold of garden-fresh spinach, and baked whole tomatoes. Mounded in the compote dish are whole spiced pears. Crisp salad greens, "all you can eat," are wheeled to the tables where guests select a dressing.

Never static, the dessert menu changes often with new pastry delights developed in Mrs. Schreiber's experimental kitchen.

ROAST CANADIAN BACON

- 4 to 5 pounds fully cooked Canadian bacon
- 1 quart unsweetened pineapple juice *or* other fruit juice
- 1 cup sugar

Remove outer wrap from roll of fully cooked Canadian bacon. Place in roasting pan and pour pineapple juice over the bacon. Bake in a 350° oven for 1 hour, spooning fruit juice over occasionally. Remove bacon (reserve pan juices) and chill for 4 hours. Add 1 cup sugar to pan juices and simmer uncovered about 10 minutes, stirring constantly until of thick sauce consistency. Spoon sauce over top of chilled bacon for a glaze. Garnish with cart wheels of orange and lime. Makes 16 to 20 servings.

CINCINNATI

Gourmet Room

The Gourmet Room, sparkling atop the twentieth floor of the Terrace Hilton Hotel, is one of Cincinnati's outstanding French restaurants. The glass window walls give a fine view in three directions of the downtown area of the city, of the Ohio River, and of some of the seven hills on which Cincinnati was built. The menu, for the most part, lists classic French dishes, done in the classic French way. They are known for their cook-at-the-table specialties such as these below.

ESCALOPES DE VEAU FLAMBEES HENRI

Place 1 pound veal, sliced very thin, between two sheets of waxed paper; flatten with mallet to ⅛ inch. Cut each slice into 3 or 4 pieces; season with salt and pepper. Melt 2 tablespoons butter or margarine in a skillet and brown meat quickly on both sides. Remove the meat to a hot platter.

Cook 1 tablespoon chopped shallots and ⅔ cup sliced mushrooms in skillet till tender but not brown. Return meat to skillet; add ¼ cup cognac and set aflame. Transfer meat, onions, and mushrooms to hot platter. Add ½ cup whipping cream and 2 teaspoons chopped parsley to skillet and warm, stirring frequently. Pour cream sauce over meat. Serve with saffron rice. Serves 3 to 4.

CAESAR SALAD, GOURMET

Melt 1 tablespoon butter in small skillet; add ⅓ cup croutons, cook and stir till slightly more brown. Remove from heat and sprinkle with garlic salt. Cool; set aside.

Rub salad bowl surface with a cut garlic clove. Add 3 anchovy fillets, 1 tablespoon olive oil, ½ teaspoon dry English mustard, and grind black pepper over. Cream mixture. Blend in 4 teaspoons lemon juice, ½ teaspoon Worcestershire sauce, and 2 tablespoons olive oil. Set aside. Place 1 egg in boiling water and let stand 1 minute. Cool slightly and break into salad bowl. Beat till dressing looks creamy. Gently toss 8 cups broken romaine with dressing. Add 2 tablespoons grated Parmesan cheese and croutons. Toss and serve. Makes 6 to 8 servings.

COLUMBUS

Marzetti's

Marzetti's Restaurant, located at 16 E. Broad Street, has a national reputation for fine food served in a pleasing atmosphere. Established in 1896, this restaurant is under the same family management today. Famous for authentic American and Italian dishes, their selection includes among other good things, spaghetti with chicken livers, Mostaccioli, Risotto, and spaghetti polpette.

One good idea sparks another. Because the guests in Marzetti's Restaurant exclaimed about the salad dressings and wanted them to be available for meals at home, in 1919 the Marzetti Company ventured into bottling its salad dressings. One taste will verify their slogan, "for America's Best Dressed Salads."

VEAL SCALLOPINE

1½ pounds veal cutlets, pounded *very thin*
⅓ cup all-purpose flour
1 teaspoon salt
1 cup fresh mushrooms, thinly sliced
½ cup olive oil
1 cup finely chopped onion
½ cup chopped celery
1 clove garlic, minced
1 tablespoon chopped parsley
1 cup beef broth
1 cup Marsala wine
¼ cup butter or margarine
¼ cup grated Parmesan cheese

Cut meat in serving pieces. Combine flour and salt; dredge meat in mixture. In large skillet, cook mushrooms in 2 *tablespoons* olive oil until tender, 4 to 5 minutes. Remove mushrooms. Add remaining olive oil to skillet and heat. Over high heat, brown pieces of veal quickly, about 1 minute per side. Use more oil if needed. Remove meat and keep warm on platter. Reduce heat. Combine next 4 ingredients in the skillet used to brown meat; cook over medium heat till light brown. Add broth and simmer 15 minutes. Add wine and simmer 15 minutes longer. Stir in butter or margarine and Parmesan cheese; add cooked veal and mushrooms. Heat through. Makes 6 servings.

DETROIT

London Chop House

Detroiters who search for the best, look to the London Chop House for the latest in gustatory pleasure. Sam and Lester Gruber, owners of this honorable restaurant, are consistent in serving the best foods their world travel has shown them how to produce. The Grubers work at keeping up to the minute with the newest and most unusual, the finest quality the culinary world can offer. Travel throughout Europe and the United States has given them firsthand exposure to the food preferences of many people. Their collection of nearly 3,000 books on food, wine, and tobacco, and of thousands of menus from all over the world provides library inspiration for constant experimentation.

Here Sam Gruber and Executive Chef Philip "Pancho" Velez attend to Cabbage Meat Rolls in Sweet-Sour Sauce. On the platter are mountainous Hamburger Steaks filled with Roquefort cheese and topped with Pancho Sauce.

PANCHO SAUCE

1 cup tomato catsup
½ cup mayonnaise
½ cup chili sauce
1 tablespoon dry mustard
1 teaspoon prepared horseradish
½ teaspoon ground ginger
¼ teaspoon monosodium glutamate
2 tablespoons pineapple juice
1 tablespoon wine vinegar
2 teaspoons Worcestershire sauce
3 drops bottled hot pepper sauce

Combine ingredients thoroughly. Serve at room temperature or heat to serve over Hamburger Steaks with Roquefort and Pancho Sauce. Makes about 2 cups sauce.

HAMBURGER STEAKS WITH ROQUEFORT AND PANCHO SAUCE

1 medium onion, chopped
3 tablespoons salad oil
2 cloves garlic, minced
2 pounds ground beef chuck
2 eggs
1 tablespoon chopped parsley
1 teaspoon salt
¼ teaspoon pepper

• • •

¼ cup crumbled Roquefort cheese
2 tablespoons soft butter
2 tablespoons brandy

Saute onion in oil until transparent. Add garlic, cook about 1 minute until garlic begins to be transparent. Add to beef. Also add eggs, parsley, salt, and pepper; mix well. Shape in 4 giant, oval hamburger balls. For filling, blend remaining ingredients until creamy. Make a deep hole on one side of each ball, fill with cheese mixture and mold the meat over the opening; repeat on the other side. Brush with oil; sprinkle with salt and pepper. Broil close to heat until sealed on both sides, finish broiling about 5 inches from heat, turning once. For medium-done, cook about 15 minutes. Serve with Pancho Sauce. Makes 4 large servings.

CABBAGE MEAT ROLLS IN SWEET-SOUR SAUCE

1 medium head cabbage
½ pound *each* ground beef and ground lamb
1 onion, chopped fine
½ cup uncooked long-grain rice
1 teaspoon salt *and* dash pepper
¾ cup water
1 can condensed beef broth
Sweet-Sour Sauce

Cook 16 cabbage leaves in boiling salted water 5 minutes or till pliable. Combine meats, onion, rice, seasonings, and water; shape lightly into 16 rolls, about 3 inches long. Place each meat roll on a cabbage leaf and roll up loosely, enclosing ends (for fluffy texture, be sure to allow room for expansion of steam). Place rolls in shallow baking dish; pour broth over. Cover with foil; bake at 350° for 1½ hours. Serve with *Sweet-Sour Sauce:* Simmer, covered, ½ cup seedless raisins in 2 cups water 30 minutes. Cook ½ cup chopped green pepper and ¼ cup chopped onion in 3 tablespoons butter till tender. Stir in ¼ cup brown sugar mixed with 3 tablespoons cornstarch. Add ½ cup wine vinegar and raisin mixture. Cook, stirring constantly, till mixture thickens and boils; cook 2 minutes. Makes 8 servings.

Huge one-half pound Hamburger Steaks with Roquefort and Pancho Sauce are shaped like a football, then filled with sophisticated Roquefort flavor.

For fluffy texture, Cabbage Meat Rolls are wrapped loosely in cooked cabbage leaves. During the baking, steam puffs the rice and expands the meat.

Marshall Field & Company

CHICAGO

Marshall Field and Company

Marshall Field's in Chicago was the first department store in this country to have a tearoom. In 1890 when the tearoom opened, menus were hand-embroidered, and sandwiches were served in baskets with little nosegays.

Today, on the seventh floor which is devoted to tearooms, and fondly called "Seventh Heaven," you can find the traditional Marshall Field's Special Sandwich pleasing hundreds of shoppers every noon. A heavenly blend of flavors, it has a rye-bread start, then stacks up with layers of white chicken meat, thin slices of Swiss cheese, and crisp lettuce. A Thousand Island Dressing concocted by Field's is ladled over and topped with a tomato-egg-slice crest.

During the Christmas season, displays at Marshall Field's are the talk of Chicago. Each year a story-book theme is captured in their famous windows along State Street. In the seventh floor Walnut Room stands a giant three-story Christmas tree surrounded by the eighth and ninth mezzanine floors. Hurried shoppers stop to relax with lunch or tea and pastries, and to admire the delicate hand-decorated ornaments hung on the boughs of the Christmas tree.

MARSHALL FIELD'S SPECIAL SANDWICH

For each serving, butter a large round slice of rye bread. Place buttered side up on a dinner plate. First put on several leaves of head lettuce, then a layer of thin slices of Swiss cheese. Add large lettuce cup, reverse side up. Cover with slices of white meat of chicken. Now pour over a Thousand Island Dressing. Top with a tomato slice, then a hard-cooked egg slice. Garnish with crisp, *hot* bacon slices, ripe olive, and topper of parsley. Makes one large serving.

BRAISED SHORT RIBS

3½ to 4 pounds beef short ribs

• • •

1¼ cups beef stock or 1 can condensed beef broth

• • •

⅓ cup all-purpose flour
3 tablespoons soft butter or margarine

• • •

1 clove garlic, finely chopped
¼ cup sherry
¼ teaspoon monosodium glutamate
Salt to taste
Pepper to taste

Brown the short ribs in a shallow baking pan in an extremely hot oven (550°) for about 15 minutes, then pour off fat.

Lower oven setting to 350°. Add the beef stock or condensed beef broth to the browned ribs and cover the pan with aluminum foil. Cook for about 1½ to 2 hours, or until the meat is tender. Skim off excess fat; reserve the broth to use in gravy. Keep ribs hot in oven while making gravy.

To make gravy, brown the flour very slowly in a skillet, then mix with the soft butter or margarine to form a paste. Stir this paste into the reserved meat broth (about 1½ cups). Cook over medium heat, stirring constantly, until gravy thickens. Stir in the chopped garlic, sherry, and monosodium glutamate. Season gravy to taste with salt and pepper.

Combine gravy and ribs, cook gently about 15 minutes longer. To serve, garnish short ribs with hot buttered baby carrots, peas, green beans, tiny parsleyed potatoes, braised onions, and broiled tomato halves (see the picture above). Serves 6 or 7.

CHICAGO

Imperial House

The kitchen performance of every dish at the Imperial House on Chicago's Gold Coast must live up to its imposing printed menu, and pass inspection by the experienced eye of Max Guggiari, owner and host. The dish under scrutiny at left is Braised Short Ribs with vegetable garnish. Imperial House salads—such as Max Salad Bowl, next page—are so famous that you may have a separate salad menu.

GRILLED MEDALLIONS OF CHOPPED BEEF TENDERLOIN

2½ pounds ground beef tenderloin
½ cup sweet cream
1 teaspoon salt
⅛ teaspoon black pepper
1 slightly beaten egg
¼ teaspoon monosodium glutamate

Combine ingredients; mix thoroughly. Use light touch to shape mixture into 4 patties. Preheat broiler to 400°. Broil patties 4 to 5 inches from heat, turning once, (3 minutes each side for rare, 5 minutes each side for medium rare, and 7 minutes each side for well done). Makes 4 servings.

Note: Ground beef chuck tastes very good seasoned and broiled this way, too.

MAISON DRESSING

1 teaspoon rich prepared mustard
1 teaspoon lemon juice
1 teaspoon Worcestershire sauce
5 tablespoons olive oil
3 tablespoons chili sauce
1 tablespoon wine vinegar
1 tablespoon drained chutney, chopped
1 cup minced water cress
Salt and Pepper to taste

Blend all ingredients well. Add salt and pepper to taste. Pour dressing into server; garnish with additional minced water cress. Pass to spoon over fruit salad.

For sea-food salad dressing: Omit chutney in above recipe. Mix the dressing with shrimp, crab-meat, or lobster salad.

An inspired Imperial House special to make at home: Max's Salad Bowl

←Leave the crusts on bread slices to make croutons like Max makes. Break bread into tiny cubes. Toast in a slow oven, stirring frequently, till dry and golden brown. Melt butter in skillet with peeled garlic clove.

Take out garlic when it is golden→ brown. Add toasted croutons and toss them until they're butter-coated. You can store a supply of these in a covered jar in the refrigerator. Heat croutons just before using.

Make dressing over crushed ice. Crumble ½ cup mild blue cheese with fork. Add 3 tablespoons light cream, ½ teaspoon rich prepared mustard, ⅛ teaspoon Worcestershire sauce, dash salt and pepper.

Stir in 2 tablespoons wine vinegar, 6 tablespoons olive oil. Have greens ready for 4—Bibb, Boston, or romaine, plus tomato wedges, peeled avocado and hard-cooked egg slices, and small artichoke hearts.

Place the salad-makings in a large salad bowl over crushed ice. Pour on the blue-cheese dressing. You "roll" this salad, not toss it. Fork in left hand goes down, spoon in right hand goes up and over salad.

When salad is well mixed, sprinkle croutons over top to add crunch. Have salad plates well chilled; carefully lift a portion of the salad to each plate—make sure everyone gets a bit of each delicious green.

CHICAGO

Cape Cod Room

The Cape Cod Room of Michigan Avenue's Drake Hotel is one of the great sea food restaurants even to a down-easter, though it's some 1300 miles from any sea. Peter Hunt, a Cape Codder himself, designed and decorated the room so that it truly captures the mood of old Salem. Marine art, lobster pot markers, hawsers, ships' wheels, compasses, and fish nets are mounted so expertly, so beautifully, and with such continuity of decor that never does it seem at all self conscious; never does one think "atmosphere." Every detail, from the captains' chairs to the dramatically lighted aquariums gives the visitor pleasure.

Sea food and fresh-water fish come fresh daily as fast as refrigerator express and jet cargo can bring them. Augmenting the seasonal fish list are 50 regular standby entries named for rivers, lakes, and oceans. Lobster itself is served at least a dozen different ways. Daily lunch specialties and chefs' suggestions exceed the number you can easily count. What's more, the chefs at the Cape Cod Room know what to do with the joys of the waters, once they get them in the kitchen, in making them into dishes of pure delight.

SHRIMPS, PILAFF

10 uncooked large shrimp, cut in thirds
2 tablespoons chopped shallots or green onions
2 tablespoons butter or margarine
⅓ cup cooked rice
Dash *each* salt and pepper

In a medium-sized skillet, gently simmer shrimp pieces and chopped shallots or green onions in butter over low heat for about 5 minutes. Add the cooked rice, salt and pepper to the shrimp mixture; mix thoroughly. Cover and cook over very low heat for about 10 minutes. Garnish with parsley and serve immediately. Makes about 2 cups pilaff.

PALMER HOUSE GRIDDLE CAKES

2 cups sifted all-purpose flour
3 tablespoons sugar
2 *tablespoons* baking powder
½ teaspoon salt
2½ cups milk
2 beaten egg yolks
2 tablespoons butter or
  margarine, melted
2 stiff-beaten egg whites
1½ cups sugar
2 tablespoons lemon juice
1 cup butter or margarine, melted
Cherry Sauce

Sift together dry ingredients. Combine milk and egg yolks; add to flour mixture; mix well. Stir in 2 tablespoons butter; fold in egg whites. Let stand few minutes. Pour ⅓ cup batter into hot lightly greased 9-inch skillet; spread to 7 inches. Cook over moderately high heat till underside is golden. Turn; brown other side. Combine 1½ cups sugar and lemon juice. Sprinkle each cake with 1 tablespoon of the lemon sugar; drizzle with 1 tablespoon melted butter. Roll as for jellyroll. Place in shallow baking dish; sprinkle with lemon sugar. Broil till sugar dissolves and becomes glossy. Pass hot Cherry Sauce. Makes about 18 7-inch cakes.

Cherry Sauce: Thaw and drain (reserve liquid) one 1-pound 4-ounce can (2½ cups) frozen red sour cherries. Combine 4 teaspoons cornstarch and ¼ cup sugar in saucepan. Gradually stir in 1 cup reserved juice. Cook and stir over low heat till juice is thick and clear. Add cherries; heat through.

CHICAGO

Palmer House

The sophistication of Chicago's Palmer House has developed through nearly one hundred years of experience. Today, seven distinguished rooms at the Palmer House serve more meals daily than any other hotel restaurant in the world. Each room presents character of its own in food and decor. Two of the most unique are the Empire Room, often called the "Room of the Stars" and the exotic South Seas Trader Vic's. Glamour accompanies each dish served at the Palmer House. Griddle Cakes come super-sized with jewel-like Cherry Sauce (left), and such classics as Shrimps de Jonghe renew their fame each time they are served.

SHRIMPS DE JONGHE

2 pounds raw unshelled shrimp
¼ cup lemon juice
1 stalk (1 piece) celery, cut up
1 small onion, cut up
2 bay leaves
¾ cup butter or margarine, softened
1 cup soft bread crumbs
¼ cup dairy sour cream
¼ cup chopped parsley
2 cloves garlic, minced
1 teaspoon Worcestershire sauce
1 teaspoon steak sauce
1 teaspoon salt
Dash freshly ground black pepper

Place unshelled shrimp in 6 cups boiling water. Add *2 tablespoons* of the lemon juice, celery, onion, and bay leaves. Cover; bring to boiling, then lower heat and simmer gently until shrimp turn pink, about 5 to 6 minutes. Remove from heat and let shrimp cool in cooking liquid. Meanwhile, cream softened butter with bread crumbs, sour cream, chopped parsley, garlic, remaining 2 tablespoons lemon juice, Worcestershire sauce, steak sauce, salt and pepper. Peel and clean cooled shrimp; place in 6 individual baking dishes. Cover shrimp with butter mixture. Bake in a hot oven (400°) for about 15 minutes or until shrimp are heated through. Serve hot. Makes 6 servings.

CHICAGO

Swiss Chalet

The Swiss Chalet in Chicago's Bismarck Hotel has long been noted for its excellent Swiss-German cuisine. Undoubtedly one of the finest offerings of this restaurant's menu is Edelweiss Torte. Layers of rich puff paste hold a velvet smooth cream filling and mountains of whipped cream. For years customers have been drawn to Swiss Chalet by this classic pastry creation.

EDELWEISS TORTE

Chill ¾ cup *plus* 2 tablespoons butter. Work with back of spoon just till pliable as putty. Roll between waxed paper to 8x6 inches. Chill 1 hour. Cut 2 tablespoons butter into 1¾ cups sifted all-purpose flour. Gradually add ½ cup ice water tossing with a fork. On lightly floured surface knead 5 minutes. Cover; let rest 10 minutes. Roll dough to 15x9 inches. Peel waxed paper from butter; place on one half the dough. Fold other half over butter; press edges of dough to seal. Wrap; chill 1 hour. Unwrap; roll to 15x9 inches. (Roll from center *just to* edges.) Brush off excess flour; fold in thirds. Turn and fold in thirds making 9 layers. Press edges to seal; wrap and chill 1 hour. Roll, fold, and chill 2 or 3 times more. Divide in 3 parts; roll each to 10-inch circle. (Use inverted plate for pattern.) Cover circles with waxed paper; stack and chill 2 to 3 hours. Prick each circle well; bake on an ungreased baking sheet at 350° for 20 minutes; cool.

Make *Cream Filling:* Combine ⅔ cup sugar, 2 tablespoons cornstarch, and ¼ teaspoon salt. Stir in 2 cups milk. Cook and stir till mixture boils. Remove from heat; stir small amount of hot mixture into 3 slightly beaten egg yolks; return to hot mixture. Cook and stir 2 minutes. Stir in 1 tablespoon butter and 1 teaspoon vanilla; cool. Make *Glaze:* Blend 1½ cups confectioners' sugar, 2 drops red food coloring, 2 drops yellow food coloring, and 2 tablespoons water. Beat together 2 cups whipping cream and ¼ cup sugar. To assemble cake place layer of puff paste on serving plate. Spread with Cream Filling. Spread next layer of puff paste with 2 cups of the whipped cream; gently place on top of Cream Filling. Top with third layer, bottom side up. Frost sides of torte with remaining whipped cream. Spread Glaze over top. Chill 45 minutes. If desired decorate top with frosting design and sides with toasted sliced almonds. Chill 2 hours before serving.

CHICAGO

Pump Room

Center of fashion; heart of elegance; eighteenth century Bath was a Mecca for English society. Here the whims and fancies of the elite were assuaged in the original Pump Room. From 1706 to 1761, Master of Ceremonies, Beau Richard Nash reigned as undisputed arbiter of elegance and manners. Under his exacting eye English aristocracy first mingled with play actors.

England's Pump Room continued in fame until it was destroyed during World War II, but in 1938 Chicagoan Ernest Byfield decided to transplant Bath, England to Chicago, Illinois. Housed in the Hotel Ambassador East, once again the Pump Room became the ultimate for society and showfolk.

To see the Pump Room in operation is to observe pageantry as colorful as any you could imagine. Against a setting of sapphire walls and white leather banquettes, waiters in hunting pink uniforms carry flaming swords of food. Coffee boys serve in emerald costume and plumed turbans. The food is a display of culinary art ranging from famous traditional dishes to the rare and exotic.

PEACHES IN FLAME

½ cup sugar
½ cup port wine
½ cup tart cherry jelly
¼ teaspoon cinnamon
Dash salt
1 tablespoon lime juice
1 1-pound 13-ounce can (3½ cups) peach halves, drained
¼ cup brandy, heated
1 quart lemon ice cream

Combine sugar, port wine, cherry jelly, cinnamon, salt, and lime juice in a blazer pan or chafing dish. Heat and stir until smoothly blended. Add peach halves, cut side down, and prick rounded surfaces with a fork. Simmer 5 minutes, basting peach halves frequently with sauce.

Add ¼ cup heated brandy, set aflame, and toss gently with silver fork and spoon until the flame dies. To serve, spoon peaches and sauce over individual servings of lemon ice cream. Makes about 8 servings.

Cold, Marinated Beef Slices. Julienne strips of cooked sirloin roast are chilled in seasoned sour cream. Garnish: pimiento and green-pepper strips, glossy ripe olive, lemon wedge.

Little Dutch-shoe Potatoes step out in culinary fashion. They're carved from partially cooked Idaho potatoes, then French-fried to crisp, golden-brown perfection and filled with buttered peas.

COLD, MARINATED BEEF SLICES

½ pound cooked sirloin steak *or* beef roast, sliced in julienne strips
1 small onion, thinly sliced and separated in rings
¾ teaspoon salt
Dash pepper
1½ tablespoons lemon juice
1 cup dairy sour cream

Combine meat, onion rings, salt, and pepper. Sprinkle lemon juice over and mix in sour cream. Chill. Serve in crystal dishes lined with leaf lettuce. Trim with strips of pimiento and green pepper. Top with ripe olive; tuck in lemon wedge. Serves 6.

STOCK YARD INN SPECIAL DRESSING

1 cup dairy sour cream
2 tablespoons mayonnaise
¼ cup light cream
½ teaspoon *each* curry powder and dry mustard
½ teaspoon Worcestershire sauce
½ teaspoon steak sauce
½ teaspoon horseradish
1 small clove garlic, minced
2 dashes bottled hot pepper sauce
Dash *each* salt and white pepper

Combine ingredients; mix well. Chill. Spoon over limestone lettuce. Makes 1¼ cups.

DUTCH-SHOE POTATOES

Choose Idaho baking potatoes about 5x2½ x2½ inches. Cook in jackets in boiling, salted water till partially done (about 20 minutes). Drain; peel. With knife, "whittle" about ½ inch off top of each, cutting slight dip in center. Round bottom slightly. "Whittle" point on one end for toe. About 1½ inches from toe, scoop out an oval about 2½ inches long and 2 inches wide, leaving ¼ inch around sides. On outside, cut off a sliver of potato near tip of toe so it turns up slightly. Shoe should be about 4 inches long, 2 wide, and 1½ high. Fry in deep, hot fat (370°) for about 3 minutes or till golden and cooked through. Drain well. To serve, sprinkle with salt; fill with hot buttered peas.

THE
STOCK YARD
INN
CHICAGO

Stock Yard Inn

"Steaks" and "broiling" are big words at this restaurant on the edge of Chicago's hustling, bustling Union Stock Yards. It all began in 1912 when cattle kings of the West came to Chicago on business and demanded the best in beef. Now world-renowned, the Stock Yard Inn keeps two fulltime butchers busy cutting meat for its diners. All beef is carefully aged four weeks—even for burgers. Inn Manager Bob Foss, and his staff, have their favorite cattlemen and take their choice of the beef animals arriving at market.

In the Sirloin Room, guests pull up a Hereford calf-hide chair. Although this is a family restaurant, the food and Western atmosphere are masculine gender. Folks ordering steak stroll over to the "steak throne" where Chef Frank Kauten displays each tender cut in all its grandeur—on silver platters kept cold on chipped ice. Diners then brand the steak of their choice with small branding irons that mark their preferred doneness. Today ninety per cent of the patrons order rare or medium-rare beef; five years ago they ordered medium or well done. Chef Kauten reveals that women are better informed than men about the kinds of steak—men are most impressed by size.

By popular demand salads and potatoes are the choice accompaniments to steak. But these are no commonplace items at the Stock Yard Inn. A Special Dressing glamorizes crisp limestone lettuce, and Dutch-shoe Potatoes filled with buttered new peas walk away with honors.

In the Postillion Room, you may dine while sitting on coach seats! Here handsome antique harnesses are the decoration reminiscent of stage coach days. Beef is king in both rooms, but it is the Sirloin Room "where the steak is born."

CHICAGO

Well of the Sea

One stair-flight below street level in Chicago's Sherman House and you're at the bottom of the ocean—or so it seems in the Well of the Sea. Underwater abstract murals, and special lighting produce an aura of being "under the sea." Its 1949 New Year's Eve opening set the pace for Well of the Sea. Often it is crowded with chic Chicago visitors and the gay friendliness is irresistible. The cuisine leans to fish and sea food of course—and here any hilarity ends. On the menu is as excellent a selection as can be found in Chicago.

OLD MR. FLOOD'S BLACK CLAM CHOWDER

¼ cup all-purpose flour
¼ cup shortening, melted
1 teaspoon curry powder
4 cups clam juice
3 cups fish stock or water
½ cup chili sauce
¼ cup tomato puree
½ cup diced celery
½ cup chopped onions
1 teaspoon salt
Pepper to taste
⅛ teaspoon saffron
⅛ teaspoon thyme
⅛ teaspoon rosemary
½ pound diced haddock
½ cup diced potatoes
¼ cup diced leeks
1½ cups minced clams
1 cup cooked tomatoes
¾ cup diced green pepper
1 clove garlic, minced
1 teaspoon monosodium glutamate
1 teaspoon chopped parsley
⅓ cup Madeira or sherry wine
12 soft shelled clams, cooked

Blend flour, shortening, and curry powder in a deep saucepan; cook 2 minutes stirring constantly. Gradually add clam juice, fish stock or water, chili sauce, and tomato puree. Cook until thickened, stirring constantly. Add celery, onions, salt, pepper, saffron, thyme, and rosemary. Simmer 15 minutes. Add haddock, potatoes, and leeks; cook 15 minutes. Add minced clams, tomatoes, green pepper, and garlic; cook 15 minutes. Remove mixture from heat; add monosodium glutamate, chopped parsley, Madeira, and cooked clams. Serves 6 to 8.

CHAMPAIGN

Uncle John's Pancake House

John P. Dahl represents a real American success story. He learned that people on the move love pancakes anytime of day. In 1956 the snowy Dutch doors of his first Pancake House in Santa Barbara, California, closed by noon the first day—not from lack of business, but because he ran out of food! Today Uncle John serves more than 15 million customers each year. Travelers need not go far to spot the familiar barn-red and white exterior of an Uncle John's Pancake House.

IOWA CORN PANCAKES WITH WESTERN CHILI

1 pound lean ground beef
1 tablespoon butter or margarine
½ envelope (about 3 tablespoons) dry onion-soup mix
2 teaspoons chili powder
¼ teaspoon garlic powder
1 1-pound can (2 cups) red kidney beans
2 8-ounce cans tomato sauce
¾ cup shredded cheddar cheese
3 eggs
1 cup sifted all-purpose flour
1 tablespoon sugar
1 tablespoon baking powder
½ teaspoon salt
1¼ cups buttermilk
2 tablespoons butter or margarine, melted
3 tablespoons yellow corn meal
½ cup whole kernel corn, drained

Brown meat lightly in 1 tablespoon butter. Stir in soup mix, seasonings, beans and liquid, and tomato sauce. Simmer uncovered 30 minutes; keep warm. Beat eggs till light and fluffy. Sift together next 4 ingredients; add to eggs. Beat till almost smooth. Stir in buttermilk and butter; beat just till smooth. Stir in cornmeal and corn. Bake (¼ cup batter for each) on hot, lightly greased griddle till golden brown. To assemble, spoon ⅓ cup meat on each pancake; fold. Top each with 1 tablespoon shredded cheese. Serve hot. Makes 10 to 12 5-inch pancakes.

Win Schuler's

JACKSON

Win Schuler's

The life and works of Charles Dickens form the central theme of Win Schuler's Jackson restaurant. On the walls of the Pickwick Room hang signs from English Inns where Dickens once visited. Historical correspondence, literature, and figures like the charming Mr. Pickwick presenting the pie at left, are also part of the decor. These things Mr. Schuler brought back from England where he visited the places familiar to Dickens and thereby developed ideas to incorporate into the decor of his restaurant. This same method he used in decorating his restaurants in Grand Haven, Michigan using a Robert Burns theme, and in St. Joe, Michigan using a Dr. Samuel Johnson theme.

Even more important to the charm, and most surely to the success of Win Schuler's restaurants, is the sincere feeling of warmth and friendliness which the Schuler clan—from manager to waitress—shows each customer. At his original restaurant in Marshall, Michigan, which Win still manages himself, he sees about 1400 customers every day and knows about half of them by name. This is true in the other restaurants, too. Guests are made to feel very welcome and at home, and they respond to the friendliness shown them by returning again and again—often driving for many miles—to have dinner at a Schuler establishment.

The food is delicious, well-served and plenteous—consider the invitation to a second helping of prime ribs with the compliments of the innkeeper! The managers of Win's four restaurants enjoy whipping up a special salad or dessert and do so often for unsuspecting, but very pleased guests. The beauty at the right was created at the Jackson restaurant and is a now favorite dessert. It's a "mile high" Grasshopper Pie, lusciously flavored with creme de menthe.

GRASSHOPPER PIE

1 cup chocolate wafer crumbs, (about 19 wafers)
¼ cup sugar
2 to 3 tablespoons butter, melted
¼ cup milk
6½ cups (¾ pound) miniature marshmallows
¼ cup green creme de menthe
2 tablespoons white creme de cacao
4 cups whipping cream, whipped

For crust, combine crumbs, sugar, and melted butter; press mixture into bottom and sides of 9-inch pie plate; cool.

For filling, combine milk, and marshmallows in top of double boiler. Heat and stir over *hot, not boiling* water till marshmallows are melted. Remove from heat; cool, stirring every 5 minutes. Combine liqueurs; add to marshmallows; blend well. Fold marshmallows into whipped cream till well combined. Fill cooled crust; freeze firm, 6 hours or overnight. Trim with whipped cream rosettes and whole fresh strawberries.

SCHULER'S HOMEMADE BREAD

2 packages active dry yeast
½ cup warm water
1¾ cups milk, scalded
¼ cup sugar
1 teaspoon salt
¼ cup salad oil
6 to 7 cups sifted all-purpose flour
2 beaten eggs

Soften yeast in water. In large mixing bowl, combine milk, sugar, salt, and salad oil. Add *2 cups* of the flour; beat well with electric mixer. Add softened yeast and eggs; beat well. Remove from mixer; add enough remaining flour to make a moderately stiff dough. Turn out on lightly floured surface; knead till smooth and satiny, 8 to 10 minutes. Cover; let rest 10 minutes. Divide into 9 balls; mound each like a bun; fold over sides and tuck in ends. Place each in a greased 5½x3x2-inch baking pan; butter tops generously. Cover; let double, about 45 minutes. Bake at 350° for 30 minutes or till done. Makes 9 small loaves.

ANGELS ON HORSEBACK

8 slices bacon
16 oysters
4 slices bread, toasted
• • •
Leaf lettuce

Cut each slice of bacon in half, then wrap a half strip of bacon around each oyster. Fry in deep hot fat (375°) for 3 minutes. Drain well on paper towels.

Cut each toast slice into fourths; arrange on leaf lettuce. Put one bacon-wrapped oyster on each piece of toast. Serve hot as appetizer. Makes 4 servings.

LANCASHIRE HOT-POT

1 lamb chop
2 ounces lamb, cubed
1 tablespoon butter or margarine
• • •
2 lamb kidneys
1 medium onion, sliced
• • •
4 fresh mushrooms, sliced
3 oysters
1 medium potato, pared and sliced
• • •
1 tablespoon all-purpose flour
½ cup beef stock
Dash salt
Dash pepper
Dash monosodium glutamate

In skillet, lightly brown lamb chop and cubes in butter; place chop in a deep individual casserole; add cubes. Halve and core the kidneys and add to the skillet with sliced onion. Cook until onion is tender but not brown; transfer kidneys and onion to the casserole. Then, add sliced mushrooms and oysters to casserole with lamb chop and cubes; top with sliced potato.

Blend 1 tablespoon flour into remaining butter in skillet; cook until brown; add the beef stock, salt, pepper, and monosodium glutamate; pour mixture over potatoes in casserole. Cover and bake in moderate oven (350°) for about 1 hour and 10 minutes. Uncover and bake 20 minutes longer to brown the potatoes. Makes 1 serving.

GRAND RAPIDS

Sayfee's

Sayfee's, housed in a store-front building near the downtown section of Grand Rapids, Michigan, offers guests an interesting selection of Syrian specialties—such as lamb pie, stuffed kibby, Yabrah, and Syrian salad—in addition to an excellent American menu. The Yabrah, or Cabbage Rolls, (below) is a tasty accompaniment dish. It's stuffed with a marvelous combination of rice, tomatoes, and ground lamb, and is subtly spiked with lemon.

YABRAH
(Cabbage Rolls)

1 large head cabbage

. . .

1 cup cooked rice
1 pound ground lamb
½ cup canned tomatoes
½ teaspoon allspice
1 teaspoon salt
Dash pepper

. . .

1⅓ cups canned tomatoes
2 cloves garlic, halved
1 teaspoon salt

. . .

¼ cup lemon juice
1 tablespoon brown sugar

Remove the thick core from center of large head of cabbage. Cook cabbage in boiling salted water, cored side down, until leaves are tender. Cut out center vein from cabbage leaves and set aside. Cut large leaves in half; leave smaller leaves whole.

Combine the cooked rice, lamb, ½ *cup* canned tomatoes, allspice, 1 teaspoon salt, and pepper, and mix thoroughly.

Place 1 level tablespoon of the meat mixture on each cabbage leaf; roll up. Place reserved cabbage veins on bottom of Dutch oven; arrange the rolls on top. Add tomatoes, garlic, and salt. Press down with an inverted dish. Cover and simmer for 1¼ hours. Add the lemon juice and brown sugar; simmer 10 minutes longer. Makes about 3 dozen cabbage rolls.

MILWAUKEE

Mader's

Enter Mader's Restaurant and such Medieval tales as Beowulf come to mind when King Hrothgar called for "a mead-hall, high and gabled," where his people could revel and make good cheer. Flaming torches light the Armour Room, one of two massive dining rooms at Mader's, and suits of armour worn by such greats as Maximilian I stand as if ready for battle. Across one end of the Armour Room hang unbelievably long lances once used in the tilt or joust, a sport of individual battle that added to the prestige of knighthood.

First opened in 1902, Charles Mader fulfilled a childhood dream when he lit the gas lamps that illuminated his restaurant. The flickering light revealed a sign that said dinner or supper included "Suppe, Kaffee, Milch or Tee" and could be had for only 20 cents. On the "Speise Karte" (menu), Milwaukeeans found a choice of German foods that included "Gebratene Schweinhaxen mit Sauerkraut" (Roast pork shank with sauerkraut), and "Sauerbraten mit Kartoffelkloessen" (Beef, marinated in wine vinegar and spices, served with potato dumplings). Cellia Mader, Charles' wife was responsible for preparing these dishes just as her mother and grandmother had done for many years in Germany.

Today Mader's Restaurant is owned and managed by Charles' very able son Gustave Mader. The standards of quality first set by his father in 1902 have been maintained and the cuisine continues to be prepared from original Old World recipes. As a director of the National Restaurant Association and president of the Wisconsin Restaurant Association, Mr. Mader has made a valuable contribution to the growth of American restaurant businesses. As a member of the world famous Confrerie de la Chaine des Rotisseurs, he has also distinguished himself as an international gourmet.

GERMAN PEASANT PLATTER

2 small pork shanks
½ teaspoon salt
¼ teaspoon pepper
¼ teaspoon garlic powder
¼ teaspoon caraway seed
3 cups water
3 Bratwurst links
3 Knockwurst links
1 1-pound can (2 cups) sauerkraut, heated and drained
Bavarian Potato Dumplings

Place pork shanks in roasting pan; sprinkle with seasonings. Pour water around, (not over), meat. Roast uncovered at 400° for 3 to 3½ hours or till done. Prick Bratwurst; broil 3 to 4 minutes on each side until golden brown. Cook Knockwurst in boiling water for 3 minutes. Arrange meats on platter around bed of hot sauerkraut as in the picture. Add hot Bavarian Potato Dumplings.

PORK TENDERLOIN WITH CREAM SAUCE

2 1½-pound pork tenderloins
⅓ cup chopped onion
½ cup chopped carrot
⅓ cup butter or margarine
1 cup beef stock or beef broth
2 tablespoons lemon juice
½ teaspoon grated lemon peel
¼ teaspoon salt
Dash pepper
¼ teaspoon thyme
1 small bay leaf
⅔ cup light cream
2 tablespoons all-purpose flour
2 teaspoons chopped parsley

Brown meat, onion, and carrot in butter. Add next 7 ingredients; cover and simmer till tender, about 40 minutes. Remove meat; slice and keep hot. Strain pan juices; measure juices and add water to make 1 cup; return liquid to skillet. Stir cream into flour; add to juices in skillet; heat and stir till mixture thickens and boils. Pour sauce over meat; sprinkle with parsley. Serve with noodles. Serves 6 to 8.

BAVARIAN POTATO DUMPLINGS

Cook 2 to 3 large Idaho potatoes in boiling salted water to cover for 40 to 50 minutes or till done; drain. Cool. Pare and put through a ricer. In a large mixing bowl combine potatoes, ¾ cup all-purpose flour, 1 slightly beaten egg, 1½ teaspoons salt, dash pepper, and ¼ teaspoon grated onion; mix thoroughly. Use ¼ cup of the mixture for each dumpling; flatten each and fill center with 3 or 4 croutons; work dough around croutons to make round ball. Drop balls into boiling salted water to cover (1 teaspoon salt to 1 quart water); simmer 8 to 10 minutes; lift out. Combine 1 cup fresh bread crumbs (about 2 slices) with 2 tablespoons melted butter; roll dumplings in crumb mixture. Serve hot. Makes 7 dumplings.

DRESDEN STYLE CHICKEN FRICASSEE

1 2½- to 3-pound ready-to-cook broiler-fryer chicken, cut up
2 teaspoons lemon juice
Salt
3 tablespoons butter or margarine
1 tablespoon flour
1 3-ounce can broiled sliced mushrooms, drained
¼ cup light cream
¼ teaspoon salt
Dash pepper
2 egg yolks
½ teaspoon lemon juice
2 tablespoons white wine

Rub chicken with 2 teaspoons lemon juice; sprinkle well with salt. Brown lightly in *2 tablespoons* butter. Add 1 cup water; steam till tender, about 45 minutes. Remove chicken; sprinkle with paprika; keep hot. Reserve broth from skillet; skim off fat. Melt remaining tablespoon butter in skillet; blend in flour. Slowly add the broth. Cook and stir till mixture boils. Add mushrooms, cream, salt, pepper. Add small amount hot mixture to egg yolks; return to hot mixture; cook and stir till thickened. Add lemon juice and wine. Serve hot over chicken on bed of buttered egg noodles. Serves 4.

MILWAUKEE

Ratzsch's

Ratzsch's offers old world charm with new world appeal and fame. Karl Ratzsch, Jr., owner, greets guests at the door while a Viennese string ensemble plays lilting old world melodies and familiar classics to assure a dulcet background for pleasant dining. Rare old steins and other antiques decorate the restaurant, and its atmosphere remains peaceful and unhurried in true romantic tradition.

APPLE STRUDEL

½ cup butter or margarine
3 cups sifted all-purpose flour
½ teaspoon salt
¾ cup warm water
1 slightly beaten egg
1 cup butter or margarine, melted
6 cups thinly sliced, pared tart apples
1 cup sugar
2 teaspoons cinnamon
½ cup currants
Sifted confectioners' sugar

Cut butter into flour and salt as for pie crust. Combine water and egg; add to flour; stir well. Turn out on lightly floured surface; knead 5 minutes. Divide in half; cover; let stand 30 minutes. Cover large table with floured cloth. On cloth, roll *half* of dough, (leave other half covered), to a 15-inch square; brush with 2 to 3 tablespoons of the melted butter; let stand few minutes. To stretch dough, use *back* of hands, working underneath dough. Start from middle of square and gently stretch from one corner to the next until dough is paper-thin (to about 36x48 inches). (Don't lift dough too high as you stretch—it tears easily!) Trim off thick edges.

Brush ¼ cup of the melted butter over the dough. Place *half* the apples evenly along one 36-inch side, about 6 inches from edge. Combine sugar and cinnamon; pour over apples; top with currants. Gently fold the 6-inch piece of dough over filling. Pick up cloth behind filling; slowly and evenly raise cloth making dough roll forward into a tight roll. Seal ends. Place on buttered 15x10x1-inch baking pan; curve slightly to form crescent. Brush top with 1 to 2 tablespoons melted butter. Repeat stretching and filling with other half of dough and filling. Bake strudels at 350° for 45 to 50 minutes. Remove from pan; cool on rack. Sprinkle with sifted confectioners' sugar.

STEPHENSON'S
APPLE FARM RESTAURANT

KANSAS CITY

Stephenson's

When twin brothers Loyd and Leslie Stephenson returned from the armed services, their ambition was to start a restaurant serving dishes their mother and grandmother made so deliciously. The family owned several orchards and sold fruit in season from a small roadside stand. Under this stand was the dirt floored cellar where crisp juicy apples were stored. Today the dirt floor has been covered and the old apple cellar is a cozy booth-lined hideaway. Other rooms have been added and there's a patio where spring guests may dine under blossoming apple trees. Plump hot apple fritters (left) rolled in confectioners' sugar are served with every meal accompanied by a huge ball of fluffy whipped butter. Moist Baked Chicken "N" Butter and Cream is Sunday dinner fare, and their special Green Rice is the rave of every man who tastes it. Throughout the restaurant is displayed one of the most unique collections of antiques in the area.

BAKED CHICKEN "N" BUTTER AND CREAM

½ cup all-purpose flour
1½ teaspoons salt
Dash pepper
½ teaspoon paprika
1 2½- to 3-pound ready-to-cook broiler-fryer, cut up
¼ cup butter or margarine
½ cup nonfat dry milk powder

Combine flour, salt, pepper, and paprika. Dip chicken in water; coat well with flour mixture. Place chicken skin side down in a 13x9x2-inch baking dish; slice butter thinly over chicken. Bake uncovered in a moderate oven (350°) for 30 minutes.

Mix dry milk powder with 1½ cups of hot water; pour around chicken. Return to oven and bake 1¼ hours longer or until chicken is tender. Remove chicken to hot platter. Makes 3 to 4 servings.

APPLE DUMPLINGS

1 cup sugar
¼ teaspoon cinnamon
¼ cup butter or margarine
1 cup water

• • •

2 cups sifted all-purpose flour
1 teaspoon salt
⅔ cup shortening
5 to 7 tablespoons cold water

• • •

6 small whole apples, pared and cored
¼ cup butter or margarine
½ cup sugar
½ teaspoon cinnamon

• • •

Whipping cream, whipped

In a saucepan, combine sugar, cinnamon, butter, and 1 cup water. Bring mixture to boiling and remove from heat.

Make pastry: Sift flour and salt together in a mixing bowl. Cut in ⅔ cup shortening with a pastry-blender or blending fork until the pieces are the size of small peas. Sprinkle 1 tablespoon of the cold water over part of flour-shortening mixture. Gently toss with a fork; push moistened part to one side of bowl. Sprinkle next tablespoon cold water over dry part; mix lightly and push to moistened part at side. Repeat until all is moistened. Gather dough up with fingers and form into a ball. On a lightly floured surface, roll the dough to a 24x16-inch rectangle. Cut in six 6- to 8-inch squares.

Place an apple in the center of each pastry square. Put 2 teaspoons butter in each apple cavity. Combine sugar and cinnamon. Reserving 2 tablespoons of sugar-cinnamon mixture, fill apples with remaining part.

Moisten edges of pastry squares. Bring corners up over top of apple and pinch together. Pinch moistened edges of pastry together. Place dumplings 1 inch apart in an ungreased 11½x7½x1½-inch baking dish. Pour cooked syrup over apples; sprinkle with reserved 2 tablespoons cinnamon-sugar. Bake in a hot oven (400°) for about 35 to 40 minutes or until apples are tender. Serve dumplings warm topped generously with whipped cream. Makes 6 servings.

GREEN RICE

3 cups cooked rice, rinsed with cold water
¼ cup finely chopped green pepper
1 cup finely chopped parsley
½ cup (2 ounces) shredded sharp process American cheese
¼ cup finely chopped onion
1 teaspoon salt
¼ teaspoon *each* pepper, seasoned salt, and monosodium glutamate
1 tablespoon lemon juice
½ teaspoon grated lemon peel
1 clove garlic, minced
¼ cup salad oil
2 beaten eggs
1 14½-ounce can evaporated milk

Combine cooked rice, green pepper and parsley. Add shredded cheese, onion, salt, pepper, seasoned salt, and monosodium glutamate. Stir in remaining ingredients. Turn into a 10x6x1½-inch baking dish. Bake in a moderate oven (350°) for 35 minutes. Remove from oven and let stand 5 minutes before serving. Serves 6 to 8.

APPLE FRITTERS

1 beaten egg
1 cup milk
1 cup finely chopped, unpeeled, cored apple (1 medium)
¼ cup sugar
¼ teaspoon salt
3 tablespoons orange juice
1 teaspoon grated orange peel
½ teaspoon vanilla

• • •

2 cups sifted all-purpose flour
3 teaspoons baking powder
Sifted confectioners' sugar

Combine first 8 ingredients. Sift flour and baking powder together; fold into egg mixture, stirring *just* till flour is moistened. Drop by rounded teaspoons into deep, hot fat (350°). When fritters rise to surface, turn and fry till deep golden brown, about 3 minutes. Drain thoroughly on paper towels; roll in sifted confectioners' sugar. Serve hot. Makes about 3½ dozen fritters.

COLORADO SPRINGS

Broadmoor

Spaciousness, comfort, old fashioned elegance typifies the Broadmoor Hotel in Colorado Springs. Located on the top floor of its newest wing is the Penrose Room. Here the height of sumptuous dining is observed in food, service, and decor. Large windows reveal a breath-taking view of the Colorado Rockies with Pike's Peak rising over 14,000 feet high. The menu offers a wide selection of classic dishes served in lavish manner. One section of the menu is devoted entirely to chafing dish specialties. While these dishes take a little longer, the experience of seeing them prepared at your table is well worth the wait.

DEVILED CRAB MEAT IMPERIAL

¼ cup butter
¼ cup *each* minced green pepper, minced onion, and minced mushrooms
2 tablespoons minced pimiento
1 tablespoon chopped shallots
2 tablespoons all-purpose flour
2 cups light cream
1 teaspoon salt
Dash pepper
1 teaspoon monosodium glutamate
½ teaspoon dry mustard
1 teaspoon Worcestershire sauce
2½ cups flaked crab meat
2½ cups dry white bread crumbs
1 cup Hollandaise Sauce

Melt butter in medium hot skillet. Add minced green pepper, onion, and mushrooms; cook until tender. Blend in pimiento, chopped shallots, and flour. Add cream and simmer 5 minutes, stirring mixture constantly. Stir in salt, pepper, monosodium glutamate, dry mustard, Worcestershire sauce, crab meat, and 2 cups of the bread crumbs (mixture will be thick). With fingers form into 8 balls. Roll balls in remaining ½ cup bread crumbs; place in individual shallow baking dishes. Bake in a moderate oven (350°) for 15 to 20 minutes. Remove from oven; top each crab meat ball with about 2 tablespoons Hollandaise Sauce. Brown under broiler for about 1 minute. Serve deviled crab piping hot. Makes 8 servings.

DES MOINES

Johnny & Kay's

Johnny and Kay Compiano are a unique Mr. and Mrs. team who started with a one room restaurant in 1946. They've stayed in the food field, expanding as business demanded to an impressive seven room establishment. Regular guests never know just what to expect in the way of decor when they visit Johnny and Kay's. Unlike many restaurants of our nation that hold to one theme for many years, the Compianos take special pleasure in surprising guests with the latest in decorating materials and furniture. But whatever the current fashion on display, it is always a tasteful combination of textures, designs, and colors.

Eating is never hurried at Johnny and Kay's—and who would want to hurry over the specialty of the house, a thick juicy steak charcoal broiled to taste on the huge grill shown at left. Johnny shrugs away the fact that he has developed some very distinctive and sought-after recipes. He calls most of them mistakes, but his "mistakes" have delighted guests for eighteen years.

JOHNNY AND KAY'S STEAK DE BURGO

2 tablespoons butter or margarine
1 garlic clove, minced
1 tablespoon sweet basil

. . .

2 4-ounce slices beef tenderloin
Salt to taste
Pepper to taste

Melt 2 tablespoons butter or margarine in a heavy skillet over high heat. Add minced garlic clove and 1 tablespoon sweet basil; cook mixture quickly until pieces of garlic are clear but not brown.

Sprinkle slices of tenderloin with salt and pepper to taste; cook tenderloin in seasoned butter to desired doneness. (For rare, cook meat about 4 minutes on each side. Allow 2 to 3 minutes longer for medium.) Serves 2.

JOHNNY AND KAY'S FRENCH-FRIED ONION RINGS

6 medium Bermuda or mild white onions, sliced ¼ inch thick
2 cups milk
3 eggs
All-purpose flour

Separate onion slices into rings. Combine milk and eggs; beat thoroughly. Follow picture directions below dipping a few rings at a time into milk, then flour. Fry a few at a time in deep, hot fat (375°) till crisp and golden brown. Remove from fat and drain on paper towels. Salt onions just before serving. Makes about 8 servings.

Pour beaten egg and milk mixture into shallow pan. Drop onion rings into pan. With fingers, swish rings around till each is well coated with liquid.

Lift onions out of liquid; shake over pan to drain. Then drop in pan of flour, a few rings at a time, coating each well. Shake off excess flour.

Fill French-frying basket ¼ full so onions will brown evenly. Set basket in deep, hot fat (375°). Stir onion rings once with a fork to separate.

When onion rings are golden-brown, remove from hot fat; drain on paper towels. To keep onions crispy, salt just before serving. Makes 8 servings.

DENVER

Brown Palace

The Palace Arms of the Brown Palace Hotel in Denver is treasured by Denverites as one of the most distinguished restaurants in the city. This dining room holds to an aristocratic atmosphere in its service and decor. Hung against the mellowed luster of dark brown paneled walls are large military prints of early American naval vessels. Surrounding these prints are flags and hand weapons of the same period. Splendid chandeliers cast a soft light over the dining room blending colors, shapes and designs.

Food at the Brown Palace is strictly American. Early every morning, fresh Rocky Mountain trout are delivered to become delicate Trout Almondine later in the day. Each year Western prize 4-H beef is purchased by the Brown Palace and from these animals are served the tenderest of beef cuts. Steaks, roasts, and ribs are cooked with the experience and care that these prime meats deserve.

TROUT ALMONDINE

6 8-ounce trout, cleaned
Salt and pepper to taste
2 slightly beaten eggs
½ cup light cream
½ cup all-purpose flour
¼ cup salad oil
¼ cup butter or margarine
½ cup slivered blanched almonds
½ cup butter or margarine, melted
2 tablespoons lemon juice

Bone whole trout; season with salt and pepper. Combine slightly-beaten eggs and cream. Dip trout in flour, then in egg and cream mixture. Heat salad oil and ¼ cup butter together. Fry trout in combined oil and butter until golden brown on both sides, about 5 minutes for each side.

Add almonds to ½ cup melted butter and cook until browned. Remove from heat; stir in 2 tablespoons lemon juice. Place trout on a warm platter; pour almond sauce over and serve immediately. Makes 6 servings.

ASPARAGUS DELICIOUS

2 pounds fresh, (*or* 2 10-ounce packages frozen), asparagus spears
1 tablespoon butter or margarine
1 tablespoon all-purpose flour
⅛ teaspoon salt
Dash white pepper
1 cup milk
½ cup shredded sharp process cheese
¼ cup slivered blanched almonds, toasted

Cook asparagus and drain. Place in warm serving dish and keep hot.

Melt butter in a small saucepan over low heat. Combine flour, salt and white pepper; blend into melted butter. Add the milk all at once. Cook quickly, stirring constantly, until mixture thickens and boils. Cook and stir 2 minutes longer. Add the shredded cheese and stir until melted. Pour cheese sauce over hot asparagus at once; top with toasted almonds. Serve hot. Serves 4.

V

GALLATIN

McDonald's Tea Room

Resembling a white-washed, plaster-of-paris doll house with gay flower-boxes and large bay windows, the stucco building which houses McDonald's Tea Room is set beside a quiet road far from a main highway in Gallatin, Missouri. The sole identification is an obscure little sign on the front of the building. Even so, for 33 years, Virginia McDonald has attracted a multitude of hungry travelers from every part of the country to her Tea Room, causing it to grow from its original counter and 3 small tables to the present capacity for 200 guests.

A unique combination of good cooking and Virginia McDonald herself tell the story of the success of the Tea Room. Her dynamic personality, her famed broad-rimmed, vegetable-laden hats and her astounding memory for names and faces have certainly played their part in bringing guests back again and again. Virginia sees to it that diners enjoy every bite. After dinner, guests settle up with her personally at her desk in the front of the room—no checks are given at the tables.

At left is a favorite dinner at the Tea Room—golden broiled chicken; crisp Potato Baskets filled with butter-sliced mushrooms, fresh peas and a touch of pimiento; and fresh Asparagus Delicious topped with a smooth cheese sauce and toasted almonds. Hot breads such as the Blueberry Muffins and Pecan Rolls are offered with every meal, accompanied by a butter rose. For dessert, try a sherbet of Virginia's popular and delicious Black Raspberry Ice. On the next page, we show easy directions for making party-pretty garnishes as they are done at McDonald's—perfect for trimming salads and other dishes.

POTATO NESTS OR BASKETS

Peel raw potatoes and shred. Select two round-bottomed, fine-meshed strainers (individual size) of different sizes. Pack potatoes on bottom and sides in large one and press smaller one on top of potatoes to hold them firmly. Then fry in deep, hot fat till golden brown. To serve, fill baskets with hot, buttered peas, butter-browned mushrooms, and chopped pimiento.

BLUEBERRY MUFFINS

2 cups sifted all-purpose flour
¼ cup sugar
4 teaspoons baking powder
1 teaspoon salt

• • •

½ cup fresh blueberries, or unsweetened, frozen blueberries, thawed and drained
1 cup milk
2 beaten eggs
¼ cup butter or margarine, melted

Sift together dry ingredients; gently stir in blueberries; make well in center. Combine milk, eggs, and butter and add all at once to dry mixture. Stir mixture quickly just until dry ingredients are moistened. Fill greased muffin pans ⅔ full. Bake muffins in hot oven (400°) for about 20 to 25 minutes or till done. Makes 12 muffins.

BLACK RASPBERRY ICE

2 quarts black raspberries

• • •

5 cups sugar
3 cups hot water
Juice of 6 lemons

Press raspberries through a colander. Then squeeze berries, through a coarsely woven cloth, extracting every possible bit of pulp but no seeds. Combine sugar and hot water in saucepan and stir until sugar dissolves. Heat to boiling; simmer 15 minutes. Combine lemon juice, raspberries and syrup; cool. Then freeze as stiffly as possible in a hand freezer. To serve, spoon into sherbets.

MCDONALD'S PECAN ROLLS

1 package active dry yeast, *or* 1 cake compressed yeast
½ cup water
1 cup milk, scalded and cooled to lukewarm
1½ cups sifted all-purpose flour

• • •

1½ cups warm water
½ cup lard, melted
2 tablespoons butter or margarine, melted
⅔ cup sugar
1 tablespoon salt
1 beaten egg
½ cup seedless raisins
½ cup finely chopped pecans
6 cups sifted all-purpose flour

• • •

1 cup brown sugar
1 cup broken pecans

• • •

½ cup butter or margarine, melted
1 cup brown sugar

Dissolve active dry yeast in ½ cup *warm* water, or compressed yeast in ½ cup *lukewarm* water. Stir in ½ *cup* of the milk; beat in 1½ cups flour. Cover dough and let rise till double, about 1 hour.

Blend in remaining ½ cup milk and the 1½ cups warm water. Stir in lard, butter, sugar, salt, egg, raisins, and chopped pecans. Gradually beat in 6 cups flour to make a soft dough. Chill dough thoroughly, 2 to 3 hours or overnight.

Divide 1 cup brown sugar and the broken pecans between 4 dozen well-greased muffin cups. Then, working with *half* the chilled dough at a time, (keep other half refrigerated), turn out on lightly floured surface; roll to 12x24-inch rectangle. Brush with ¼ *cup* of the melted butter; sprinkle with ½ *cup* of the brown sugar. Roll as for jellyroll, beginning with long side; seal edge. Cut into 1-inch pieces. Place rolls, cut side down over nut mixture in muffin cups. Cover and let rise till double, about 1 hour. Repeat with other half of dough. Bake rolls in moderate oven (350°) for 25 to 30 minutes or till done. Turn out of pan at once. Serve warm, pecan side up. Makes about 4 dozen rolls.

Add spring to salads with perky flower garnishes—easy directions below.

Calla lilies. Choose big, smooth white turnips. Let stand at room temperature 1 day. Pare. Cut thin slices (round and round, not letting knife point go beyond center of turnip). Cut carrot stamens.

Curve a slice in left hand; insert carrot stamen. Curve another slice in right hand. Slip over petal in left hand until flower can be held in left. Push toothpick through base. Crisp in cold water.

Shasta daisies. Cut thin turnip slices. Cut holes in slices; insert carrot curls. Then, cutting to within ¼ inch of carrot, make 20 petals; cut thin wedge from right side of each of the petals.

Snip off ends of petals making a diagonal cut as shown. We used the plain end of a small metal cake decorating tube to cut the perfect round holes. A paring knife or kitchen scissors would do.

Zinnias. Use 3 turnip slices varying ⅓ inch in size. Make 12 petals in each; round corners. Stick pick into 1-inch carrot stamen, then through smallest turnip slice, next size, and largest. Push together.

Marigolds. Thinly slice large carrots. Cut small carrots into 1- to 1¼-inch lengths; cut each in half, then in thirds, for stamens. Stick pick through a slice, then a stamen. Cut petals; round corners.

LEA & PERRINS

HOTEL
Mayfair
ST. LOUIS

Mayfair Room

Dark woods, with a lustrous patina, old prints, and the tinkle and shimmer of crystal candelabras give the Mayfair Room a stately, while comfortable, appearance. This hotel dining room in St. Louis, Missouri, is under the able direction of Mrs. Julia King. A lady of glamour, Mrs. King uses the combination of excellent food and dependable service to attract her clientele.

And attract them she does with such excellent dishes as Steak Diane, Mayfair, pictured on the opposite page. Fittingly named after the Goddess of the Hunt, this prime sirloin cut is described on the menu as seared and sauteed in butter, in close union with shallots and mushrooms—and aflame with brandy.

STEAK DIANE, MAYFAIR

1 10-ounce sirloin steak, about
 1 inch thick
Butter

. . .

2 dry shallots, finely chopped *or*
 2 tablespoons finely chopped onion
4 fresh mushroom caps, sliced

. . .

1 teaspoon Worcestershire sauce
2 tablespoons brandy

Trim almost all the fat from steak. Preheat a skillet or blazer pan of chafing dish until hot enough to sizzle a drop of water. Add just enough butter to prevent sticking. Brown the steak quickly on one side, about 1 minute. Reduce heat. Add shallots and sliced mushrooms; cook 2 minutes. Turn; cook over medium heat about 6 minutes longer or to desired degree of doneness. Add Worcestershire and brandy.

To ignite sauce, pull blazer pan to edge of chafing dish flame and tilt slightly away from you, or light with a match. Slide the pan back and forth while blazing to blend the sauce well. When flame is about extinguished, remove meat to a heated plate and spoon the sauce (or drippings) over steak. Garnish with water cress and serve with baked potato or wild rice. Serves 1.

Charlie's
cafe exceptionale

MINNEAPOLIS

Charlie's Café Exceptionale

Charlie's Café Exceptionale, situated in the heart of the Minneapolis downtown area at 701 Fourth Avenue, is a meeting place for lovers of good food from Minnesota, or from any part of the country.

Charlie's made restaurant history when it was the first to present a before-dinner appetizer tray, an inspiration of owner Charles Saunders. The revolving smörgåsbord tray is now the high spot of dinner as it is set in the center of the table loaded with delicacies (note the silver tray shown in the background of the picture at left). Guests help themselves at the spin of the tray to scoops of Liver Pâté, smoked turkey, icy relishes, and many other specialties.

Another of Charlie's good ideas: As soon as diners are seated, a bowl of Charlie's Potato Salad, and a dish of pickled herrings are brought to the table to keep them happy while ordering and waiting to be served.

The menu at Charlie's is varied and sophisticated. You have your choice, for example, of his well-known planked steak, Cornish hen, Midwest frog's legs, sea food flown in from both oceans, and superb Chicken Kiev. Opposite, in the Hunt room, Chef Mahlke, an expert's expert, chats with Manager Harold Ahlman about the merits of Roast Peppered Rib Eye of Beef. A favorite with Charlie's patrons, they laud the robust spicy flavor of this tender beef dish. Special Wild Rice is a wonderful accompaniment when you're serving it at home.

For Roast Peppered Rib Eye of Beef, rub pepper and cardamom over all, pressing with heel of hand.

In a large bowl, mix the ingredients for Charlie's Potato Salad gently, then chill *at least* 2 hours.

ROAST PEPPERED RIB EYE OF BEEF

Have fat trimmed from a 5- or 6-pound boneless rib eye beef roast. Marinate as directed. Combine ½ cup coarsely cracked pepper and ½ teaspoon ground cardamom seed; rub all over beef and press in with heel of hand. Place in shallow baking dish; carefully pour over this sauce: Mix 1 tablespoon tomato paste, ½ teaspoon garlic powder, and 1 teaspoon paprika; gradually add 1 cup soy sauce, then ¾ cup vinegar. Refrigerate overnight—spoon marinade over meat.

Remove meat from marinade; let stand at room temperature 1 hour. Wrap in foil; place in shallow pan; roast at 300° for 2 hours for medium-rare. Open foil; ladle out and reserve drippings. Brown roast uncovered at 350° while making gravy. Strain drippings; skim off excess fat. To 1 cup meat juices, add 1 cup water; bring to boiling. If desired, add a little marinade. Serve *au jus* or thicken with 1½ tablespoons cornstarch mixed with ¼ cup cold water. Serves 8 to 10.

SPECIAL WILD RICE

Rinse 1½ cups wild rice thoroughly; combine with 4 cups water, 1 teaspoon salt, and 1 small onion. Cover and simmer till tender, 40 to 45 minutes. Remove onion; drain rice in colander. Dice 4 strips bacon; fry until crisp; add 4 finely chopped green onions, and 6 thinly sliced fresh mushrooms; cook just until tender. Add drained rice; season with salt and freshly ground black pepper. Heat through. Makes 6 servings.

CHARLIE'S POTATO SALAD

5 medium potatoes, pared and freshly cooked
1 teaspoon salt
Dash white pepper

. . .

2 tablespoons chopped green onions
2 tablespoons chopped pimiento
3 hard-cooked eggs, diced
1¼ cups mayonnaise
¼ cup diced celery

Dice the potatoes, (makes about 5 cups when diced), and spinkle with the salt and pepper. Add remaining ingredients and mix gently. Season to taste with salt and pepper. Chill at least 2 hours. Makes 8 servings.

LIVER PÂTÉ

½ cup chopped onion
1 clove garlic, minced
⅓ cup rendered chicken fat

. . .

1 pound chicken livers
1 teaspoon salt
¼ teaspoon pepper
Dash thyme

Cook onion and garlic in chicken fat until tender but not brown. Add chicken livers, salt, pepper and thyme. Cover and cook slowly until livers are cooked through but not crisp. Put mixture through food chopper using fine blade. Whip until smooth, then chill. To serve, garnish with chopped egg and onion. Makes about 1½ cups.

Chateau de Paris

MINNEAPOLIS

Chateau de Paris

Very French in decor as well as cuisine, the Chateau de Paris in the Hotel Dyckman is reminiscent of that gay city. Walls of the "Wine Keg" are lined with barrels from an underground "Chais" in Burgundy. The oval casks and lanterns in the "Cave" or wine cellar, were brought from France also, and guests in the "Cafe", main dining room of the Chateau, dine under chandeliers like those which hung above the grand Parisian society parties at the turn of the century.

ORANGE SAUCE

2 oranges
4 cups water

• • •

⅓ cup sugar
1 tablespoon vinegar
¼ cup lemon juice

• • •

3 tablespoons butter
2 tablespoons flour
2 cups veal or beef broth
¼ cup cognac
¼ cup kirsch
2 tablespoons cornstarch
2 tablespoons water

With knife, score peel of oranges lengthwise in narrow strips. Use vegetable parer to shave off several strips at a time. Place peel in boiling water; simmer 15 minutes. Drain; pat dry with paper towels. Remove white membrane from oranges; section and reserve for garnish. Combine sugar and vinegar. Cook and stir till mixture caramelizes, about 5 minutes. Stir in lemon juice and orange peel. In a saucepan, blend butter, flour, and cornstarch. Stir in meat broth, cognac, kirsch, and caramelized mixture. Cook and stir till mixture boils; cook 1 to 2 minutes longer. Serve with roast duckling. Garnish duck with reserved orange sections. Makes 3 cups sauce.

STILLWATER

Lowell Inn

Mrs. Nelle Palmer owns and manages one of the most charming restaurants in the United States. Since 1930, the Palmers have put artistry into each detail of Lowell Inn, located in Stillwater, Minnesota, developing superb recipes and spotlighting foods on precious china and crystal.

The Matterhorn Room, newest of the dining rooms at Lowell Inn, contains a rare form of art. One of the few remaining masters of wood carving, Edward Blatter, came from Switzerland to lend his talent and experience to the creation of this room. Across one wall is a striking mural of the Matterhorn and Zermatt village—an 8-inch thick relief carving made of white grainless African mahogany. Only one meal is served in this room. Its star is a Swiss classic, Fondue Bourguignonne. Sizzling hot oil and cubes of the tenderest beef are brought to the table. With long-handled forks, guests cook away to their own taste. Then the meat is dipped in a number of elegant sauces for a variety of delectable flavors.

FONDUE BOURGUIGNONNE

2 pounds beef tenderloin, cut in 1x2-inch pieces
Salad oil for cooking

Pour oil in a beef-fondue cooker or deep chafing dish to depth of about 1½ inches. Heat to 425° on range. Take hot oil to the table; place over alcohol burner or canned heat. Have beef cubes at room temperature in a serving bowl. Pass small bowls of Bearnaise Sauce, Bordelaise Sauce, Caper Sauce and Anchovy Butter. At the table each guest cooks a beef cube in the hot oil with a long-handled fork to desired doneness. The cooked meat is then dipped into one of the sauces on his plate. When oil cools so that meat no longer cooks briskly, heat again on range. Makes 3 to 4 servings.

BEARNAISE SAUCE

6 egg yolks
1 cup butter or margarine, melted
2 tablespoons tarragon leaves
2 teaspoons chopped shallots
¼ cup tarragon vinegar
¼ cup dry white wine
1 cup mayonnaise

Beat egg yolks slowly till thick and lemon colored. Beat in ½ *cup* of the butter. Combine tarragon leaves, shallots, and vinegar; simmer 5 minutes. Remove from heat; stir in wine. Place egg yolk mixture in top of double boiler over *hot, not boiling* water. (Water should not touch bottom of pan.) Slowly add remaining ½ cup butter, stirring constantly. Cook and stir just till mixture thickens. Remove from heat; blend in wine mixture. Add mayonnaise; mix well. Makes 2 cups.

BORDELAISE SAUCE

½ cup fresh mushrooms, chopped
1 tablespoon butter or margarine
3 tablespoons cornstarch
2 cups beef stock
1 tablespoon tarragon leaves
2 tablespoons lemon juice
3 tablespoons red wine
Dash pepper

Saute mushrooms in butter till tender, about 4 minutes. Stir in cornstarch; gradually add beef stock. Cook and stir till mixture boils. Add remaining ingredients; simmer 15 to 20 minutes. Makes 2¼ cups.

CAPER SAUCE

In a small mixing bowl combine 1 cup mayonnaise and 1 tablespoon undrained capers. Serve with Fondue Bourguignonne.

ANCHOVY BUTTER

With electric mixer, beat together 2 cups butter, one 2-ounce can anchovy fillets, and 2 tablespoons chopped parsley. On waxed paper, form mixture into 2 long rolls, 1 inch in diameter. Chill at least 1 hour. To serve, cut slices ⅓ inch thick.

DEVONSHIRE GREEN GRAPES

3 cups seedless green grapes
½ cup dairy sour cream
Dark creme de cacao *or* brown sugar

Wash grapes and drain thoroughly. Add sour cream; mix carefully, coating grapes well. Chill at least 2 hours. To serve, turn into glass sauce dishes; pass creme de cacao or brown sugar. Makes 6 servings.

LUSH STRAWBERRY MERINGUE PIE

3 egg whites
¼ teaspoon cream of tartar
1 cup sugar
4 cups fresh strawberries, cleaned and halved
2 cups whipping cream
¼ cup sugar

Beat egg whites and cream of tartar *just* till soft peaks form. Gradually add 1 cup sugar, beating to stiff peaks. Spread in a 9-inch pie plate, mounding sides high. Bake in very slow oven (275°) for 60 minutes. Turn oven off; leave meringue in oven till it cools. Fill shell with half the strawberries. Whip cream with ¼ cup sugar. Spread over strawberries in shell; garnish with remaining berries. Chill pie well, 3 to 4 hours; serve in wedges.

RIBBON CAKE FROSTING

4 cups sugar
1 teaspoon cream of tartar
4 stiff-beaten egg whites
2 teaspoons vanilla
Few drops red food coloring

Combine sugar, cream of tartar, and 1½ cups water. Cover; boil for 3 minutes. Uncover and cook to *between* a soft and firm ball (240°). Pour syrup slowly into egg whites, beating constantly with electric beater or wooden spoon. Add vanilla and red food coloring to give very delicate tint. Beat until of spreading consistency. Frosts tops and sides of four 9-inch layers.

Here's the cake you've always dreamed about! Four stories high, each story is a different, luscious flavor. On the bottom is rich chocolate cake, then comes a feather-light, lemon layer, then peppermint, then white cake. Frosting's delicate pink, spread between layers and swirled on top and sides.

RIBBON CAKE

Lemon and chocolate layers:

½ cup shortening
1½ cups sugar
2 eggs
2¼ cups sifted cake flour
2½ teaspoons baking powder
1 teaspoon salt
1 cup plus 2 tablespoons milk

• • •

½ teaspoon lemon extract

• • •

1½ 1-ounce squares unsweetened chocolate, melted and slightly cooled
1 tablespoon milk

Thoroughly cream shortening and sugar; add eggs; beat until fluffy. Sift together dry ingredients; add alternately with 1 cup plus 2 tablespoons milk to creamed mixture. Pour half the batter into another bowl. Add lemon extract to one half of batter. Mix together slightly cooled chocolate and 1 tablespoon milk; blend into other half of batter. Pour each into a paper-lined 9x1½-inch round pan. Bake in a moderate oven (375°) for 25 minutes or until done.

Silver and pink layers:

5 egg whites
½ cup sugar
⅔ cup shortening
1¼ cups sugar
1 teaspoon vanilla
2⅔ cups sifted cake flour
3 teaspoons baking powder
1 teaspoon salt
1 cup milk

• • •

⅛ teaspoon peppermint extract
Few drops red food coloring

Beat egg whites until foamy. Add ½ cup sugar gradually, beating only until soft peaks form. Thoroughly cream shortening, 1¼ cups sugar, and vanilla. Add sifted dry ingredients alternately with milk. Stir in beaten egg whites until well blended. Flavor half of batter with peppermint extract and tint a delicate pink with red food coloring. Pour each batter into a paper-lined 9x1½-inch round pan. Bake in a moderately hot oven (375°) for 30 minutes or until done. When all layers are cool, frost between layers and on top and sides with Ribbon Cake Frosting. Makes 20 servings.

SCHIMMEL

OMAHA

Blackstone Hotel

The Orleans Room in the Blackstone Hotel is the Schimmel Brothers' answer to requests from Omaha diners for a pleasing combination of delicious food, fine wines, and excellent service. Especially popular with loyal Blackstone patrons are the Sunday morning brunch and evening buffet. Both are serve-yourself-style, and you are welcome to seconds—and thirds, if you think you can!

Here is a dinner specialty of the Orleans Room—Breast of Chicken "Perigourdine." Tender, boned chicken breasts make an attractive and delicious dish served with hot broccoli, parsleyed potatoes, and a creamy rich sauce over all.

BREAST OF CHICKEN "PERIGOURDINE"

3 boned whole chicken breasts
3 tablespoons butter or margarine
1 cup chicken broth

. . .

3 tablespoons butter or margarine
¼ cup all-purpose flour
1 cup light cream

. . .

Broccoli spears, cooked and drained
Tiny boiled parsleyed potatoes

Brown chicken breasts in 3 tablespoons butter. Place in 9x9-inch baking dish; add chicken broth. Cover and bake in moderate oven (375°) for 1 hour or till tender. Remove chicken, (reserve broth); place on ovenproof platter; keep warm. Melt 3 tablespoons butter in small saucepan; blend in flour. Stir in reserved broth and cream. Cook and stir until mixture thickens and boils. Season to taste with salt and pepper. Arrange hot broccoli and potatoes around chicken on platter; pour some sauce over and pass remainder. Serve hot. Serves 4.

GRAND TETON NATIONAL PARK, JACKSON

Jackson Lake Lodge

Nestled at the foot of Wyoming's Grand Teton Mountains, Jackson Lake Lodge offers a vacation home that appeals especially to families. Its natural grandeur is like a Cinerama movie—snow-capped mountains rising straight up from beautiful Jackson Lake, and the flower-splashed Alpine meadow.

Since the Grand Teton National Park and Jackson Lake Lodge were gifts to the United States from John D. Rockefeller, Jr., it is operated on a nonprofit basis. This accounts for the moderate cost of rooms and meals.

General Manager Raymond C. Lillie believes that "good food away from home is very important." Of course his philosophy sounds great to guests with sharpened mountain-air appetites. For breakfast, stacks of pancakes, waffles, and crisp curly bacon fortify everyone for the morning's hikes and rides.

Luncheon and dinner menus rival the variety and perfection of those in big-city hotels. Steaks sizzle on high charcoal broilers; desserts are fresh daily from the lodge's own bakeshop. And in keeping with the wilderness country, elk salami and buffalo meat are occasionally served!

At a chuck-wagon dinner, as pictured on the opposite page, superbly seasoned Chuck-wagon Stew fills the copper chafing dish. Garden vegetables snap with freshness, and dessert is hearty Apple Turnovers with big cups of campfire coffee. All the while, the giant picture window (60 feet long!) of the Main Lounge offers a breath-taking mural of the Tetons, Jackson Lake, and the meadow.

SALAD STYLING

At the Lodge, salads are "built up," never flat as a pancake. To give this lift, Chef Blum serves salads in frilly double lettuce cups or atop a bed of shredded lettuce. He stands tomato slices on edge like cart wheels for a third-dimensional look.

For tossed salads, all vegetables are in big pieces—identifiable, beautiful, fresh.

ROQUEFORT DRESSING

Use 1 part cream cheese to 2 parts Roquefort cheese. Blend the softened cheeses; then add to your favorite French dressing till it reaches the consistency you prefer.

CHUCK-WAGON STEW

2 pounds beef chuck, cut in 1½-inch cubes
2 teaspoons all-purpose flour
2 tablespoons fat

• • •

2 teaspoons salt
¼ teaspoon pepper
1 teaspoon sugar
1 teaspoon chili powder
¼ teaspoon thyme
1 bay leaf
2 tomatoes, quartered
1 green pepper, cut in coarse pieces
1 cup beef stock, *or* 1 can condensed beef broth
1 cup water

• • •

6 small potatoes, pared and halved
6 small carrots, halved
6 small whole onions
3 or 4 stalks green celery, cut in large slices
1 cup fresh peas

Dust meat lightly with flour; thoroughly brown on all sides in hot fat, turning often. Add next 10 ingredients. Cover; simmer over low heat till meat is almost tender, 1½ to 2 hours, stirring occasionally to keep from sticking. Add potatoes, carrots, onions, and celery. Cover; cook 30 minutes longer. Add peas; cook 15 minutes more or till vegetables are done. Serves 6 to 8.

APPLE TURNOVERS

1 recipe Rich Pastry
2 cups finely chopped tart apples*
½ cup sugar
1½ to 2 teaspoons cinnamon
1 tablespoon butter
Light cream

• • •

Sifted confectioners' sugar

In center of each square of Rich Pastry, place about ¼ cup of the chopped apple. Combine sugar and cinnamon and sprinkle over apples. Dot with butter. Brush edges of pastry with cream; fold over in triangles and seal edges well. Cut a few slits in tops and brush lightly with cream.

Place on aluminum-foil-covered baking sheets. Bake in very hot oven (450°) for 20 to 25 minutes or until nicely browned. Sift confectioners' sugar over tops. Serve warm. Makes 8 turnovers.

*If apples are not tart, add a few drops of lemon juice after chopping.

RICH PASTRY

2 cups sifted all-purpose flour
1 teaspoon salt
⅔ cup shortening
5 to 6 tablespoons cold water

• • •

3 tablespoons slightly softened butter

Sift together flour and salt. Cut in shortening with pastry-blender or blending fork until pieces are the size of small peas.

Sprinkle 1 tablespoon of the water over part of the flour-shortening mixture. Gently toss with fork; push to one side of bowl. Sprinkle next tablespoon water over dry part; mix lightly and push moistened part aside. Repeat until all is moistened.

Gather up with fingers; form dough into a ball. On lightly floured surface, roll to 20x10-inch rectangle, about ⅜ inch thick. Dot with 2 tablespoons of the butter; fold dough in thirds crosswise. Dot with remaining butter and fold into thirds again. Roll to 20x10-inch rectangle. Cut into eight 5-inch squares for Apple Turnovers.

TETON FRENCH TOAST

Cut day-old bread slices into tall triangles to resemble Teton peaks (see picture at right). Combine 1 cup milk, 2 well-beaten eggs, and ¼ teaspoon salt. Dip bread into egg mixture; fry in hot fat till golden brown. Sift confectioners' sugar on peaks. Serve hot with butter, maple syrup, and currant jelly.

Hot Teton French Toast calls for plenty of butter and syrup. Serve with juice, prunes, and crisp bacon.

FUDGE SAUCE

½ cup light corn syrup
1 cup sugar
3 1-ounce squares unsweetened chocolate
1 teaspoon vanilla
½ cup evaporated milk or whipping cream

Combine corn syrup, sugar, and 1 cup water. Cook to soft-ball stage (236°). Remove from heat and add chocolate; stir until chocolate melts. Add vanilla. Slowly stir in evaporated milk; mix well. Chill. Makes 1¾ cups. For *Fudge De-lights* split cupcakes in half and fill with pink peppermint ice cream. Spoon Fudge Sauce over top.

It's a Fudge De-light! Spoon rich Fudge Sauce over sandwich of party pink ice cream and cupcake slices.

CHEF BLUM'S CREAMY TETON DRESSING

⅓ cup tarragon vinegar
1 tablespoon mixed pickling spices
1 bay leaf
1 to 3 teaspoons sugar
¾ teaspoon salt
Dash white pepper
1 teaspoon paprika
½ teaspoon dry mustard
2 egg yolks
1 cup salad oil

Combine vinegar, pickling spices, and bay leaf; heat just to boiling. Remove from heat; let steep few minutes. Strain out spices, reserving vinegar. Combine sugar, salt, pepper, paprika, and mustard; add egg yolks. Blend in the vinegar, mixing well. Slowly add salad oil, beating with mixer or rotary beater, until ¼ cup has been added. Pour in remaining oil in increasing amounts, beating until thick and well blended. Serve with fruit salad. Makes about 1½ cups.

Serve fruit topped with whipped-cream mayonnaise from pineapple shell. Pass Creamy Teton Dressing.

DAVEN HAVEN HAM LOAF

1 cup milk
1 cup dry bread crumbs
2 slightly beaten eggs
2 pounds ground smoked ham
1½ pounds ground lean pork

Combine ingredients well. To shape, pack in 10x5x3-inch loaf pan, then invert on a shallow baking pan. Score top with handle of wooden spoon, or knife. Bake at 350° for 1½ hours. Baste occasionally with *Brown-sugar Glaze:* Combine ¾ cup brown sugar, ¼ cup water, ¼ cup vinegar, and 2 teaspoons dry mustard. Serve with Horseradish Sauce. Makes 12 servings.

Horseradish Sauce: Mix ¼ cup horseradish, 1½ tablespoons vinegar, 1 tablespoon prepared mustard, ½ teaspoon salt, 4 drops Worcestershire sauce, and dash *each* of cayenne and paprika. Whip ½ cup whipping cream. Fold horseradish mixture into whipped cream; chill. Serve with ham, beef, or tongue. Makes 1 cup sauce.

DAVEN HAVEN

GRAND LAKE

Daven Haven

Rib-sticking meals are the forte of Daven Haven in Grand Lake, Colorado. After a day of horseback riding, swimming, and sailing, guests find that owners Mr. and Mrs. Lester Piper know just how to cope with mountain-air appetites. A special for the small fry is the traditional hobos' hike. Armed with a lunch in red bandanna, and bottled beverage in hip pocket, they're off to see the wonders of nature—and to feed the chipmunks.

A Daven Haven special is robust Ham Loaf (at left). Basted with sweet-sour Brown-sugar Glaze, this meaty red dish glistens with moistness. Served with tangy Horseradish Sauce, all the goodness of ham is accented. Other mountain fare includes puffy spoon bread and rich stew. For dessert peaches and cherries share the tender piecrust blanket of Deep-dish Peach Pie.

DEEP-DISH PEACH PIE

¼ cup all-purpose flour
¼ teaspoon *each* salt and nutmeg
3 cups sliced sweetened peaches
¼ cup drained maraschino cherries, cut in half
1½ tablespoons butter
1 tablespoon maraschino-cherry syrup
1 recipe Rich Piecrust

Combine flour, salt, and nutmeg. Add peaches and cherries; toss lightly to blend well. Turn into 10x6x1½-inch baking dish. Dot with butter; sprinkle with cherry syrup.

Prepare *Rich Piecrust:* Sift together 1 cup sifted all-purpose flour and ½ teaspoon salt. Cut in 3 tablespoons shortening until mixture resembles corn meal. Cut in 3 tablespoons lard until pieces are the size of small peas. Sprinkle 1 tablespoon cold water over part of mixture; gently toss with fork and push to one side. Repeat until all flour is moistened. Form dough into ball. Let stand several minutes. On lightly floured surface, roll in 9x6-inch rectangle. Cut in 3-inch squares with pastry wheel. Cut small hole in center of each square. Place squares over fruit. Bake at 425° for 35 minutes, or until pastry is crisp and nicely browned. Serve warm with ice-cream curls. Serves 6.

Chicken Salad—white meat in big tender chunks

Baur's Chocolate Torte boasts triple rich flavor

Fast work makes ruffly Pecan Shell sundae dishes

CHOCOLATE TORTE

¼ cup shortening
1 cup sugar
2 egg yolks
2 1-ounce squares unsweetened chocolate, melted
1¼ cups sifted all-purpose flour
½ teaspoon *each* salt, baking powder, soda
¾ cup milk
1 teaspoon vanilla
2 stiff-beaten egg whites

Stir shortening to soften. Gradually add sugar, creaming thoroughly. Add egg yolks one at a time, beating well after each addition. Stir in melted chocolate. Sift together flour, salt, baking powder, and soda. Add to creamed mixture alternately with milk and vanilla, beating well after each addition. Fold in egg whites until well-blended. Spread into 2 paper-lined 9x1½-inch round pans. Bake at 350° for 18 to 20 minutes. Cool; spread Truffle Filling between layers. Top with Chocolate Glaze.

TRUFFLE FILLING

8 1-ounce squares semisweet chocolate
1 cup whipping cream
½ cup slivered blanched almonds, toasted

Melt chocolate over hot water; cool slightly. Whip cream just till *soft* peaks form. Fold in chocolate and toasted almonds. Mixture should be smooth and dark.

CHOCOLATE GLAZE

1½ 1-ounce squares unsweetened chocolate
2 tablespoons butter or margarine
1½ cups sifted confectioners' sugar
1 teaspoon vanilla

Melt chocolate and butter over low heat, stirring constantly. Remove from heat. Stir in confectioners' sugar and vanilla until crumbly. Blend in 3 tablespoons boiling water; add more water as needed, a teaspoon at a time (takes about 2 teaspoons), to form medium glaze of pouring consistency. Pour quickly over top of Torte; spread glaze evenly over top and sides.

DENVER

Baur's

Denver was a rough and tumble mining town when Otto Baur arrived in 1857. A baker by trade, he used his profession to good advantage and soon opened a shop of his own. Gold had provided new wealth to Denver, and hostesses reacted with a flutter of entertaining. Mr. Baur soon found his food in great demand.

Especially popular were his desserts. One day Mr. Baur persuaded a regular customer to try soda pop with ice cream. It was great—and before the end of that year, the Ice Cream Soda was a national rage.

Today Baur's offers a selection of dishes made famous through the years. Each creation reflects a combination of experience and good taste.

PECAN SHELLS

2 tablespoons butter or margarine
½ cup brown sugar
1 slightly beaten egg
¼ cup very finely chopped pecans
⅓ cup sifted all-purpose flour
¼ teaspoon vanilla
Few grains salt

Cream butter and sugar. Add remaining ingredients; mix well. Chill. *Make 1 cooky at a time keeping batter chilled when not in use.* For each put 1 rounded tablespoon on very *well-greased cold* baking sheet; spread to 3½-inch circle. Bake at 350° about 7 minutes. Cool 30 seconds. Remove from baking sheet; *immediately* shape over bottom of custard cup or glass. Makes 6 to 8.

BAUR'S CHICKEN SALAD

1¾ cups cubed, cooked breast of chicken*
1¾ cups chopped celery
1 cup mayonnaise
2 tablespoons lemon juice
Salt
Pepper

Combine cooked chicken and celery. Blend mayonnaise and lemon juice; add to chicken. Mix ingredients lightly. Season to taste with salt and pepper. Serve in lettuce-lined salad bowls. Garnish salad with sliced, stuffed olives and water cress as shown in the picture. Makes 5 servings.

*For moist, full-flavored chunks of chicken, cool stewed chicken in the rich stock.

"COOKIE'S" CORN FRITTERS

1 cup sifted all-purpose flour
2 teaspoons baking powder
½ teaspoon salt
2 well-beaten eggs
¾ cup light cream
1 1-pound can (2 cups) cream-style corn
¼ cup butter or margarine, melted

Sift together dry ingredients. Blend remaining ingredients; add to flour mixture; stir just till moistened. Fry in greased skillet; use ¼ cup batter for each fritter. Turn once when top is bubbly and few bubbles have broken. Add extra fat as needed. Makes 16 fritters. To serve, top with *Hard Sauce:* Cream ½ cup butter and 2 cups sifted confectioners' sugar till fluffy. Beat in 1 egg, 2 tablespoons brandy and ¼ teaspoon vanilla. Chill. Spoon on fritters; sprinkle with nutmeg. Makes 1⅓ cups sauce.

CELERY-SEED SALAD DRESSING

1 cup sugar
1½ teaspoons all-purpose flour
1 tablespoon paprika
¼ teaspoon dry mustard
½ cup vinegar

• • •

1 tablespoon celery seed
2 teaspoons onion juice

• • •

1 cup salad oil

In saucepan combine sugar, flour, paprika, and mustard. Stir in vinegar. Bring mixture to boiling over medium heat, stirring constantly. Remove from heat; cool. Add celery seed and onion juice. Add oil in slow stream, beating constantly with electric or rotary beater. Do *not* refrigerate. Stir well before using. Serve over fresh avocado and citrus fruit slices. Makes about 1½ cups.

KR

TUBAC

Kenyon Ranch

The tradition of relaxed Southwest living is a habit at Kenyon Ranch in Tubac, Arizona. Each evening cowboys build a moonlight campfire of fragrant mesquite brush. Mealtime brings such pleasures as delicious, crisp Corn Fritters (left) with fluffy Hard Sauce. A drizzle of Celery-seed Dressing over avocado and citrus fruit makes a perfect complement. Birthdays are special here too—celebrated with a grand Rancho Birthday Cake decorated with Western brands.

RANCHO BIRTHDAY CAKE

1½ cups sugar
½ cup shortening

• • •

1 teaspoon vanilla
2 eggs
2¼ cups sifted cake flour
2½ teaspoons baking powder
1 teaspoon salt
1 cup milk

Gradually add sugar to shortening, creaming thoroughly. Add vanilla. Beat in eggs, one at a time. Add sifted dry ingredients alternately with milk, mixing well after each addition. Pour into 2 paper-lined 9x1½-inch round pans. Bake in moderate oven (375°) for 25 minutes or till done. Cool. Frost with "Lazy-K" Frosting; decorate tops and sides with Western ranch "brands" of Chocolate Confectioners' Sugar Frosting.

"LAZY-K" FROSTING

1½ cups sugar
Dash salt
¼ teaspoon cream of tartar
4 stiffly beaten egg whites
1½ teaspoons vanilla

Cook and stir sugar, dash salt, cream of tartar, and ½ cup water over low heat till sugar dissolves. Cover 3 minutes to dissolve crystals on sides of pan. Uncover; cook to very-hard-ball stage (265°). Add syrup slowly to egg whites, beating constantly (8 minutes). Add vanilla; beat till soft peaks form.

CHOCOLATE CONFECTIONERS' SUGAR FROSTING

Melt ½ of 1-ounce square unsweetened chocolate. Add 4 teaspoons milk and 1¼ cups sifted confectioners' sugar; mix well.

TUCSON

Old Adobe Patio

Built in 1868, the Old Adobe Patio was first home to the owner of Tucson's liveliest saloon. Many luxuries graced its rooms—among them the first zinc bathtub to be found in a private home. Today Old Adobe Patio is a state historic site owned by the Arizona Pioneers' Historical Society. Fig, pomegranate, orange, and palm trees shade the patio where guests enjoy Mexican and American specialties. Layered in colors of the Mexican flag, Almendrado (below) is one of the few authentic Mexican desserts. Surprisingly light and delicate with crunchy bits of almond, Almendrado makes a refreshing finale to traditionally hot Mexican meals.

ALMENDRADO

1 envelope unflavored gelatin
½ cup cold water
4 egg whites
¾ cup sugar
Dash salt
2 drops almond flavoring
2 drops red food coloring
11 drops green food coloring
⅓ cup whole blanched almonds, ground

Soften gelatin in cold water. Dissolve over hot water. Chill until partially set. Whip egg whites until soft peaks form. Gradually add sugar and salt beating until stiff peaks form. Beat gelatin and almond flavoring into egg whites. Divide mixture evenly into 3 bowls. Color one part pink, one green, and add ground almonds to third part. Pour in layers in 8½x4½x3-inch baking dish, (almond mixture in center). Chill until firmly set (about 3 hours). To serve, turn out on plate; slice. Pass Custard Sauce. Serves 9.

CUSTARD SAUCE

6 egg yolks, slightly beaten
¼ cup sugar
Dash salt
2 cups milk
¼ teaspoon almond flavoring

Combine first 3 ingredients. Add milk gradually, stirring constantly. Cook and stir over *hot, not boiling* water till sauce coats a metal spoon. Remove from heat; add almond flavoring. Chill. Makes 2⅓ cups.

SANTA FE

La Fonda

Situated in the oldest state capital in the United States, La Fonda captures the atmosphere of Santa Fe Trail days while offering the most modern conveniences. A blend of Indian, Spanish, and Anglo-American cultures produces a beauty that soon becomes a special kind of enchantment to La Fonda visitors. Sweeping earth-colored terraces are arranged pueblo fashion and guest rooms are uniquely furnished with rare pieces from Spain and Mexico. Winter finds skiing enthusiasts flocking to Santa Fe. Nearby, the peaks of Sangre de Cristo Mountains rise to 12,200 feet and are rated among the twelve top ski spots in the United States. Foods at the La Fonda again reflect the influence of old Mexico. Their Santa Fe Omelette (below), is sauced with cheese and peppered with green chiles.

SANTA FE OMELETTE

½ cup shredded sharp process American cheese
Dash paprika
¼ cup light cream
2 eggs
1 canned peeled green chile, diced
Salt to taste
Pepper to taste

In top of double boiler, melt cheese with paprika and cream over *hot, not boiling,* water. Keep warm. In mixing bowl, beat eggs lightly with a fork; add diced green chile, salt, and pepper. Heat an 8-inch skillet (kind with flared sides is best for omelet-making). Add 1 teaspoon butter—it should sizzle and brown *lightly.* Tilt pan to grease sides. Pour in omelet mixture, leaving heat moderately high. With fork tines up and parallel to skillet, rapidly stir through top of uncooked egg. Keep omelet an even depth. As you stir the uncooked egg zigzag fashion, out to edges, the cooked bits will come to center. Shake pan all the while to keep egg mixture moving. Omelet cooks in 2 to 3 minutes. When egg is set but still shiny, remove pan from heat. Spoon part of cheese mixture across center of omelet; flip sides over, envelope style to hold in cheese. Roll omelet onto plate and top with remaining cheese mixture. Makes 1 serving.

CHEZ LOUIS

CHEZ LOUIS

SCOTTSDALE

Chez Louis

Louis Germain didn't have to pioneer in introducing good food to Scottsdale, Arizona. His loyal patrons were there ready and waiting—some of the most traveled people in the country and most comfortable in their way of living. They don't want big chandeliers and plush bars; they just want good food and they know when they've found a man who specializes in specialties.

Chez Louis is located behind a disarming little rancho shop front. Modest and unassuming, it fits into a row of almost identical fronts shaded by a low block-long canopy. Hitching posts and bumper logs that separate the street from the walk give evidence of Scottsdale's resistance to bigness and impressiveness.

Louis, formerly with Perino's in Los Angeles, wanted to move far away from clanging city tensions and from a city of tinsel and glitter. It is clear that a man of his talents had to have a place of his own. Here food is cooked as French people like it—simple, unpretentious, with the savor and succulence of expertly blended flavors. Apparently that's the way Scottsdale people like it, too, for tables are crowded noon and night. The menu is not large—that is, not so large that Louis can't improvise and improve whenever he pleases. Entrees are each prepared to order, and it's a sure bet that Louis has had a hand someplace in the preparation. Pictured at left are two of the most popular entree dishes, Coq au Vin and Shrimps Nino Nello.

For dessert, French pastries are perishably fresh each day and impossible to resist. Another beautiful dessert creation is Creme Caramel, pictured at the left, a delicate velvet-smooth custard reversed from a mold and garnished with perfect whole strawberries perched in peaks of whipped cream.

SHRIMPS NINO NELLO

1½ pounds large raw shrimp, peeled and deveined (about 2 pounds in shell)

• • •

¼ cup lemon juice
1 cup olive oil
½ cup finely chopped onion
2 garlic cloves, minced
3 shallots, finely chopped
¼ cup finely snipped parsley

Combine all ingredients; let marinate in refrigerator for 1 day. Drain shrimp. Place in a shallow baking pan. Bake in a hot oven (400°) for about 15 minutes. Serve immediately. Makes 8 to 10 servings.

STEAK MARCHAND DE VIN

2 teaspoons butter or margarine
2 teaspoons all-purpose flour
1 cup beef broth or consomme

• • •

1 tablespoon chopped mushrooms
3 tablespoons Burgundy

• • •

⅓ cup cognac
1 teaspoon finely chopped shallots
½ bay leaf
Dash thyme
2 peppercorns
1½ pounds sirloin steak

In a saucepan, melt butter and blend in flour. Cook and stir over low heat till mixture browns. Add beef broth or consomme and bring mixture to boiling; cook 3 minutes, stirring constantly. Then lower the heat and simmer for about 20 minutes.

In another saucepan, combine mushrooms and Burgundy; simmer till liquid is reduced to ½, about 5 minutes. Stir in brown sauce and remove from heat.

In a third saucepan, combine cognac, shallots, bay leaf, thyme, and peppercorns. Cook till all liquid evaporates. Add mushroom mixture; stir to blend. Remove bay leaf and peppercorns. Place sirloin steak in a heavy skillet; cook quickly on both sides. Add 2 tablespoons cognac and set aflame. Pour sauce over and serve. Serves 2.

COQ AU VIN

4 strips bacon, cut in small pieces
2 tablespoons chopped onion
1 2½- to 3-pound ready-to-cook broiler-fryer chicken, cut in pieces

• • •

8 shallots or small whole onions
½ cup coarsely chopped carrots
1 clove garlic, minced
2 tablespoons cognac
1 pint fresh mushrooms, sliced
2 tablespoons butter or margarine

• • •

3 to 4 sprigs parsley
1 medium bay leaf
¼ teaspoon dried thyme leaves *or* 1 teaspoon fresh thyme leaves
2 to 3 sprigs celery leaves
2 cups red Burgundy

In a skillet, brown bacon pieces and chopped onion; remove. Add chicken pieces and brown slowly in bacon drippings; remove. Add shallots or small whole onions, carrots, garlic, and cognac; cook till tender, about 3 minutes. Cook mushrooms in 2 tablespoons butter or margarine.

Make Bouquet Garni: In a tea ball or cheesecloth bag combine the parsley, bay leaf, thyme, and celery leaves. Place in a 2-quart casserole. Arrange the chicken pieces, vegetables, and sliced mushrooms in layers. Add Burgundy to the skillet; heat to boiling and stir to loosen the crusty brown. Pour mixture over casserole. Cover and bake in a moderate oven (350°) for 2 hours. Remove the Bouquet Garni from the casserole before serving. Makes 4 servings.

ZABAGLIONE AU MADERA

6 egg yolks
½ cup sugar
¼ cup Chablis wine
¼ cup Madeira wine

With an electric mixer, beat together egg yolks and sugar till very thick and lemon colored, 3 to 4 minutes. Gradually beat in Chablis and Madeira. Cook over *hot, not boiling* water till mixture becomes smooth and thick. Makes 4 to 6 servings.

CREME CARAMEL

2 cups milk
4 slightly beaten egg yolks
2 slightly beaten eggs
½ cup sugar
½ teaspoon vanilla
½ cup sugar

Scald milk and cool slightly. Combine next 3 ingredients; slowly stir in milk. Add vanilla; set aside. In a heavy skillet, stir ½ cup sugar over low heat till melted. When golden brown remove from heat. Pour syrup into a 3-cup ring mold; swirl to coat bottom and sides. Pour custard into mold. Set in shallow pan on oven rack; pour hot water around mold 1 inch deep. Bake in 325° oven 1¼ hours, or till knife inserted off-center comes out clean. Chill. Garnish with whipped cream and strawberries. Serves 6.

BEEF BOURGUIGNONNE

3 pounds beef chuck, cut in 1½ inch cubes
⅓ cup all-purpose flour
¼ cup butter or margarine
¼ cup olive oil
¼ cup cognac
• • •
3 slices bacon, cut in small pieces
8 small carrots
6 small onions
2 leeks, chopped
1 clove garlic, minced
1 cup red Burgundy
1 cup beef broth
12 small mushroom caps
1 tablespoon butter or margarine
½ pound (8) small onions
¼ cup red Burgundy
Snipped parsley

Dredge beef cubes in flour. In a large skillet brown beef on all sides in ¼ cup hot butter or margarine and olive oil. Set cognac aflame and add to browned beef cubes. When the flame burns out place the mixture in a casserole dish or Dutch oven and set aside.

In same skillet cook and stir bacon, carrots, onions, leeks, and garlic until bacon is crisp and vegetables are lightly browned. Drain and place mixture in the casserole with the meat. Add 1 cup red Burgundy and the beef broth. Cover and simmer for 1 to 1½ hours or till tender.

In small skillet cook mushroom caps in 1 tablespoon butter or margarine till tender, about 2 to 3 minutes. Remove mushrooms and set aside. In same skillet, brown ½ pound onions and add ¼ cup red Burgundy. Cook mixture 30 minutes or till tender.

Just before serving, place the cooked onions and mushrooms on top of the casserole. Heat mixture thoroughly. Sprinkle the top with snipped parsley. Serve with boiled potatoes or buttered noodles. Serves 8.

PATE MAISON

2 cups sifted all-purpose flour
½ teaspoon salt
½ cup butter or margarine
1 beaten egg
3 to 4 tablespoons ice water
• • •
½ pound pork, ground
¼ pound veal, ground
2 ounces liver, ground
¼ cup lard
1 teaspoon salt
Dash pepper
2 tablespoons cognac
⅓ cup Madeira
• • •
½ cup consomme

Sift together flour and salt; cut in butter. Add egg and enough ice water to moisten mixture; toss with fork to mix. Wrap dough in waxed paper and chill overnight.

Blend next 4 ingredients to a smooth paste. Stir in next 4 ingredients. Roll chilled dough on floured surface to 10x5 inches. Line a pate mold or 9½x5x3-inch loaf pan, leaving a ¾ inch edge of dough around top. Fill with meat mixture. Roll remaining dough to 10x6 inches; place atop meat. Fold over edge of dough; crimp edge. Cut a ½-inch round hole in top of dough; insert a small paper funnel. Bake in 350° oven for 1 hour. Drain fat from funnel; cool. Pour consomme in hole. Chill thoroughly before serving. Serve in 1-inch slices.

SUN VALLEY

Sun Valley Lodge

This beautiful mile-high resort represents America's glamour capital of "skidom." Here experts and snow bunnies alike gather for relaxation, fun, good food—and skiing. In 1936 the world's first ski lifts mounted Sun Valley's slopes. Engineers of the Union Pacific Railroad (owners of Sun Valley) designed these lifts that take skiers a thrilling 6,000 feet high. Late in the season, spring turns this land into crystal magic when tanning-strength sun shines on powdery snow.

Each afternoon tea calls for a break at Sun Valley Lodge. With just a hint of formality, this is an occasion in the traditional European style. A plaidjacketed waiter draws hot, fragrant brew from a huge copper tea urn while the table offers moist dainty sandwiches of turkey, ham, or Swiss cheese. For dessert, trays are laden with an array of rich French pastries and Fruit Tarts. One bite into these delicacies reveals the pudding and cake surprises created by Pastry Chef Bill Mallory. Dinner continues with Tyrolean flavor at a sister restaurant, the Ram. A yodeler's special, Swiss Pie surrounds Swiss cheese, onion, and crisp bacon bits with a custard filling. Hungarian Goulash over noodlelike Spätzles captures the quality of gourmet fare to satisfy the most distinguishing appetite.

Evenings, the lilt of music stirs tapping feet. Chairs group cozily around a blazing fire for lively chatter about the day's adventures and conquests in the mountains. Besides skiing, the skating rink, an outdoor warm-water swimming pool, and plenty of sledding invite the young at heart—whatever their age.

SUN VALLEY ECLAIRS

½ cup butter or margarine
1¼ cups sifted all-purpose flour
½ teaspoon salt
5 eggs

Combine butter and 1 cup water; bring to boiling. When butter has melted blend in flour and salt, stirring rapidly, until mixture forms a ball that does not separate, about 1 minute. Add eggs one at a time beating vigorously after each till smooth. Drop by heaping tablespoons on greased baking sheet spreading each to 4x1-inch eclairs. Or, place dough in pastry bag to form long eclairs. Bake at 450° for 15 minutes; reduce heat to 325°, bake 25 minutes longer. Remove eclairs from oven; split. Turn oven off; put back in oven to dry out, about 20 minutes. Cool on rack. Just before serving, fill centers with Pastry Cream Filling (about ¼ cup for each). Replace tops; frost with Chocolate Glaze. Makes 12.

PASTRY CREAM FILLING

¾ cup sugar
¼ cup cornstarch
¾ teaspoon salt
3 cups milk
3 slightly beaten eggs
3 tablespoons butter or margarine
1½ teaspoons vanilla

Combine first 3 ingredients. Gradually blend in milk. Cook over medium heat, stirring constantly, till mixture thickens and boils; cook 2 minutes longer. Stir a little of hot mixture into eggs; stir into remaining hot mixture. Stirring constantly, bring just to boiling and cook 1 minute longer. Add butter and vanilla. Cool. Makes 3¼ cups.

CHOCOLATE GLAZE

1½ 1-ounce squares unsweetened chocolate
2 tablespoons butter or margarine
1½ cups sifted confectioners' sugar
Dash salt
1 teaspoon vanilla
3 tablespoons boiling water

Melt chocolate and butter over low heat. Remove from heat; add confectioners' sugar, salt, and vanilla. Gradually beat in boiling water till glossy and of spreading consistency. Frost tops of filled eclairs.

FRUIT TARTS

2 cups sifted all-purpose flour
1 teaspoon salt
⅔ cup shortening
5 to 7 tablespoons cold water
• • •
1 recipe Pastry Cream Filling
8 to 10 2-inch rounds of white *or* yellow cake, sliced ¼ inch thick
1½ cups drained fresh stewed or canned pear halves, peach slices, *or* pineapple chunks
1 recipe Apricot Glaze

Sift together flour and salt. Cut in shortening until pieces are size of small peas. Sprinkle water over mixture *1 tablespoon at a time* until all is moistened. With fingers form into a ball. On lightly floured surface, flatten ball slightly and roll to ⅛ inch thickness. Cut in 6-inch circles; fit pastry into tart pans, pressing out air bubbles. Trim edges; flute. Prick bottoms and sides well. (Or fit pastry circles over inverted custard cups; pinch corners together; prick well.) Bake at 450° about 7 minutes or till golden. Cool shells.

To make Fruit Tarts, spoon about 3 tablespoons Pastry Cream Filling in each shell. Place a 2-inch round of white or yellow cake over the filling; top with drained, fresh stewed or canned fruit. Spoon a rounded tablespoon of Apricot Glaze over top of each tart. Makes 8 to 10.

APRICOT GLAZE

1½ cups apricot halves, sieved
¾ cup sugar
1 tablespoon light corn syrup
• • •
1 tablespoon lemon juice

Combine apricot pulp, sugar, and syrup in a small saucepan. Simmer about 20 minutes or until mixture is as thick as whipping cream. Blend in lemon juice.

SWISS PIE

6 slices bacon, cut in ¼-inch strips
1 cup chopped onion (about 2 medium)

. . .

2 beaten eggs
¾ cup dairy sour cream
½ teaspoon salt
Dash pepper
12 ounces Swiss cheese, shredded (about 3 cups)

. . .

6 unbaked 4-inch tart shells
Chopped chives (optional)

Fry bacon until crisp. Drain on paper towels; add onion to fat and cook until tender but not brown; drain off fat. Combine eggs, sour cream, salt, pepper, cheese, onion, and bacon. Pour into tart shells. Bake in moderate oven (375°) about 25 minutes, or until knife inserted halfway between outside and center of filling comes out clean. Garnish with chopped chives, if desired. Serve at once, one pie to each person or cut wedges and serve as an appetizer. Makes 6 small pies.

HUNGARIAN VEAL GOULASH

2½ pounds veal, beef, or pork, cut in ½-inch cubes
¼ cup fat
1 cup chopped onion (about 2 medium)
1 clove garlic, minced
¼ cup all-purpose flour
1½ tablespoons paprika
1½ teaspoons salt
¼ teaspoon pepper
¼ teaspoon thyme
2 bay leaves
1 No. 2½ can (3½ cups) tomatoes
1 cup dairy sour cream

Brown meat, half at a time, in hot fat. Reduce heat; add onion and garlic; cook until onion is tender but not brown. Blend in flour and seasonings. Add tomatoes. Cover; simmer, stirring occasionally, until meat is tender, about 1 hour. Stir often toward end of cooking. Stir in sour cream; remove from heat. To serve, spoon over hot, buttery Spätzles. Makes 6 to 8 servings.

SPÄTZLES

2 cups sifted all-purpose flour
2 eggs
2 egg yolks
⅔ cup milk
1 tablespoon minced parsley
1¼ teaspoons salt
Dash pepper
Dash nutmeg

. . .

¼ cup butter or margarine
½ cup soft bread crumbs

Combine flour, eggs and yolks, milk, parsley, salt, pepper, and nutmeg. Place mixture in a coarse-sieved colander. Hold over large kettle of rapidly boiling salted water; press through colander with a heavy-bottomed glass, lightly greased to prevent sticking. When all mixture has been pressed through colander, cook for about 5 minutes, stirring occasionally. Wash under cold water; drain.

Melt butter in pan; add bread crumbs and brown lightly. Stir in spätzles and brown lightly over low heat. (Some extra chopped parsley and chopped hard-cooked egg may be added for garnish just before removing the spätzles from heat.) Makes 6 servings.

It's rich Hungarian Veal Goulash with Spätzles—a flavorful old world favorite. After supper, Lodge guests are invited to brand their names right on the table!

OLIVE OIL

SEATTLE

Canlis

Patrons of Canlis Charcoal Broiler Restaurant can be sure of excellent food prepared from the finest ingredients. The head chef, Joe Ching, coordinates menus and recipes among all three Canlis' restaurants, located in Seattle, Portland, and Honolulu. The Seattle restaurant, opened in 1950, is a contemporary-style building of gray stone and dark stained wood. Its location high above Lake Union allows one of the most dramatic views of city lights and water to be found in Seattle. Diners may look through windows to see tier upon tier of sparkling lights that climb the hills surrounding the dark water of the lake. Each table is softly lighted by a copper-shaded candle; room lights are held to a minimum so the drama of the setting becomes a part of the enjoyment of the dinner.

Guests are deftly served by pretty Japanese girls wearing bright colored kimonos. A high point of any Canlis dinner is the pleasure of watching them prepare a Canlis Special Salad from a cart next to the table. With no apologies to Caesar the salad contains mixed greens tossed with croutons, minced bacon and grated cheese. All is blended with a dressing of lemon juice, olive oil, a coddled egg, and freshly ground pepper. Other specialties at Canlis are charcoal broiled steaks and chops prepared at the huge, copper-hooded broiler that's a dining room focal point. And a Canlis baked potato is a production in itself. It's freshly baked and topped with butter, sour cream, chopped green onions, Romano cheese, and bacon crumbles. Just as delicious are the poached shrimp and king crab legs served with mock hollandaise sauce. With coffee at the end of a delectable dinner, a cleverly folded napkin containing bright foil-wrapped candies is placed in front of each guest, a pleasant ending to a wonderful dinner.

RUSSIAN SOUP

1 10½-ounce can (1⅓ cups) condensed consomme
¼ cup dairy sour cream
1 teaspoon buttermilk
2 teaspoons red or black caviar
Lemon wedges

Chill consomme well. Combine dairy sour cream and buttermilk. To serve, spoon chilled consomme into 4 small stemmed glasses. Top each serving with about 1 tablespoon sour cream and ½ teaspoon caviar. Garnish with lemon wedges. Serves 4.

CANLIS FRENCH DRESSING

½ cup olive oil
½ cup red wine vinegar
Dash salt
Dash freshly ground black pepper
½ clove garlic
¾ teaspoon chopped fresh mint *or* ¼ teaspoon dried mint
½ teaspoon oregano

Place all ingredients in a bottle or cruet. Allow mixture to stand in the refrigerator for 2 hours. Remove clove of garlic. To serve, shake vigorously and pour generous amount over crisp, cold greens. Makes 1 cup.

CANLIS SHRIMP

2 tablespoons olive oil
2 tablespoons butter or margarine
2 pounds (about 40) large prawns, *or* shrimp, in shell
½ teaspoon salt
½ teaspoon fresh ground black pepper

• • •

2 tablespoons lemon juice
¼ cup dry vermouth

Blend olive oil and butter in large skillet over medium heat. Add shrimp, salt and pepper; cook shrimp till golden red and well done, about 5 minutes. Add lemon juice and vermouth; continue cooking over high heat for one minute, stirring constantly. Serve hot as an appetizer or an entree.

CANLIS SPECIAL SALAD

2 tablespoons olive oil
Salt
1 large clove garlic
2 tomatoes, peeled and cut in eighths
2 medium heads Romaine, sliced in 1-inch strips
¼ cup chopped green onion
½ cup freshly grated Romano cheese
1 pound bacon, fried crisp and finely chopped

• • •

1 recipe Canlis Special Dressing
1 cup croutons

Into a large wooden salad bowl pour 2 tablespoons olive oil, sprinkle with salt and rub bowl firmly with a clove of garlic. Remove garlic. Place tomato pieces in the bottom of the bowl; add sliced Romaine. Add chopped green onion, freshly grated Romano cheese, and finely chopped fried bacon.

When ready to serve drizzle *Canlis Special Dressing* over the salad following a Z-line for even distribution of the dressing. Add croutons last. Roll-toss to mix well. With the salad spoon in your right hand and the salad fork in your left hand, go down to the bottom of the bowl with one tool while going up and over with the other. "Roll" the salad until every leaf shines with dressing. (This will keep all the salad in the bowl. Not even a leaf flies out.) Serve *at once* on chilled plates. Makes 4 to 6 very generous servings.

CANLIS SPECIAL DRESSING

⅓ cup olive oil
⅓ cup lemon juice
¾ teaspoon chopped fresh mint, *or* ¼ teaspoon dry mint
¼ teaspoon freshly ground black pepper
¼ teaspoon oregano
1 egg

In a small bowl combine olive oil, lemon juice, mint, freshly ground black pepper, and oregano. Place egg in boiling water, turn off heat and let stand 1 minute. Add coddled egg to oil mixture and whip vigorously. Drizzle over Canlis Special Salad.

SEATTLE

Ivar's

In 1946 on Seattle's old Pier 54 at the foot of Madison Street, Ivar Haglund opened Ivar's Acres of Clams. It is a unique place where happy folks meet to dine on the wonderful tidbits of the sea. While clam nectar and steamed clams are the heart of the menu, just about every kind of sea food is available. Ivar's is famous for halibut, salmon, dungeness crab, Alaska shrimp, and tiny Olympia oysters hauled fresh from cold, cold waters and cooked to diners' specifications.

The view of the restless sound is always dramatic and constantly changing. Seattle's fireboats purr in and out as their port is right next door.

KODIAK SANDWICH

½ cup dairy sour cream
1 tablespoon finely snipped chives
1 tablespoon finely chopped celery
Dash garlic salt
4 slices rye bread
6 ounces (about 1 cup) king crab meat, flaked

Blend sour cream, 1½ *teaspoons* of the chives, celery, and garlic salt. Spread each slice of bread with 2 tablespoons of the sour cream mixture and top with about ¼ cup crab meat. Garnish with remaining chives; chill. Makes 8 open-faced sandwiches.

BARBECUE DIP FOR CRAB

¼ cup *each* tomato sauce, tomato catsup, and chili sauce
3 tablespoons brown sugar
3 tablespoons vinegar
1 teaspoon *each* dry mustard, barbecue spice, and garlic salt
½ teaspoon bottled steak sauce
2 fresh or frozen crabs, thawed

Combine all ingredients except crab; simmer about 15 minutes, stirring occasionally. Cook crab in boiling water allowing 8 minutes for each pound of crab. Clean and cut into large pieces. Serve hot with dip.

SEATTLE

Rosellini's Four · 10

At Rosellini's the emphasis is on continental cooking. Many of the dishes are either prepared or sauced from chafing dishes at the table. Here, Mr. Victor Rosellini is giving the finishing touches to Tagliarini Verdi Con Fungi al Burro. On the Lazy Susan is an appetizer tray of pickled cici beans, thin slices of salami, Italian antipasto, and Pate Maison in the center. To the left is a plate of Prosciutto with Artichokes. At the left front is Rex Sole Saute Amandine—sole sauteed in a delicately flavored almond sauce, and at center front is Tournedos of Beef Della Casa with Bearnaise Sauce—a succulent steak with a rich sauce.

TAGLIARINI VERDI CON FUNGI AL BURRO

1 12-ounce package Tagliarini noodles

. . .

3 tablespoons butter or margarine
2 tablespoons Parmesan cheese
½ pound fresh sliced mushrooms, cooked *or* 1 6-ounce can sliced mushrooms, drained
¼ cup light cream
Fresh ground black pepper to taste
Parmesan cheese

Cook noodles in boiling salted water about 12 minutes or till tender; drain well. Place noodles in a large bowl and add remaining ingredients. Mix well. Serve hot with additional cheese. Makes 4 to 6 servings.

PROSCIUTTO AND ARTICHOKES

Drain one can or jar of artichoke hearts packed in water or oil. Wrap a paper-thin slice of Prosciutto (Italian ham) around each artichoke heart. Serve as an appetizer.

TOURNEDOS OF BEEF DELLA CASA

- 4 large fresh mushroom caps
- ¼ cup butter
- ¼ cup olive oil
- 4 fillets of beef, about 2 inches thick, (6 to 8 ounces each)
- Salt and pepper to taste
- 4 thin slices Prosciutto
- 4 slices enriched white bread, toasted
- ½ cup Bearnaise Sauce

In a skillet cook mushroom caps in butter and olive oil for about 3 minutes. Remove from skillet and add fillets; cook for about 10 minutes, turning to brown all sides evenly. Remove to 10x6x1½-inch baking dish. Top each fillet with 1 slice Prosciutto and a mushroom cap. Bake in a moderate oven (350°) for 5 minutes. Cut toasted bread to size of fillets. To serve: Place each fillet on a slice of toast; top each with about 2 tablespoons Bearnaise Sauce. Makes 4 servings.

REX SOLE SAUTE AMANDINE

- ¼ cup all-purpose flour
- 1 teaspoon salt
- ¼ teaspoon pepper
- 4 rex soles
- 1 tablespoon olive oil
- ¼ cup butter
- ¼ cup chopped almonds
- 1 tablespoon lemon juice
- 1 tablespoon snipped parsley

Combine first 3 ingredients; coat fish. Fry in hot olive oil 7 minutes per side, or till fish flakes. Remove from pan. Melt butter in skillet, mixing with crusty bits. Add almonds, lemon juice, and parsley; cook and stir till brown. To bone fish: With tip of a sharp knife, carefully cut the full length, about ½ inch in from back and down to spine. Ease this strip back. Following same cut, slither knife flat along spine to loosen flesh; gently fold this piece down so both sides are spread out. Sever head; carefully lift out spine, leaving fine bones attached to it. Pick out strays. Flip fish back together. Repeat with other fish. Serve hot with sauce. Makes 4 servings.

CANNOLI

- ¼ pound veal, cut in ½ inch cubes
- ½ pound beef, cut in ½ inch cubes
- ¼ cup chopped onion
- 1 garlic clove, minced
- ½ teaspoon lemon peel
- 2 tablespoons butter or margarine
- 1 10-ounce package frozen chopped spinach, cooked and drained
- Dash thyme
- Dash pepper
- ½ teaspoon salt
- 2 beaten eggs
- 16 pieces manicotti (large macaroni about 1 inch in diameter), cooked
- 1½ cups tomato sauce
- ½ cup Parmesan cheese

Cook first 6 ingredients together for 20 minutes. Add spinach and put mixture through the fine blade of a meat grinder. Season with thyme, pepper, and salt. Add eggs; mix well. Put mixture in a pastry bag and fill each piece of manicotti. Arrange side by side in a 10x6x1½-inch baking dish. Cover with tomato sauce. Bake in 350° oven 10 minutes. Sprinkle with cheese and brown under broiler for 2 minutes. Serves 8.

FRITTATA

- 4 slices bacon, diced
- 1 cup zucchini, chopped
- 1 10-ounce package frozen (1 cup) chopped spinach, cooked and drained
- ¼ cup chopped onion
- ½ teaspoon salt
- Dash pepper
- Dash oregano
- 6 eggs
- 2 tablespoons Parmesan cheese

Cook bacon; drain. Add zucchini, spinach, and onion. Stir well; cook for about 5 minutes. Season with salt, pepper, and oregano. Beat eggs till fluffy; add Parmesan cheese. Pour vegetable mixture into eggs; mix well. Return entire mixture to frying pan; cover and cook over low heat till slightly browned on bottom, about 5 minutes. Place in moderate oven (350°) for 10 minutes. Loosen omelet; slide onto warm platter. Serves 4.

SAN FRANCISCO

Kan's

As long as there has been a San Francisco, there have been epicurean treats in its Chinatown. One of the outstanding restaurants is Kan's, at 708 Grant Avenue, in the heart of colorful Chinatown. Kan's maitre d' will gladly lead an untutored guest through the intricacies of the Cantonese cuisine. The menu includes just about everything from a first course of Sea Weed Soup or Bird's Nest Soup to a dessert of Chilled Lichees or Sesame Cookies. And, too, they offer the ultimate in banquet-style Chinese food—a nine course Peking Duck Dinner.

SWEET AND SOUR PORK
(*Goo Low Yuke*)

½ cup all-purpose flour
½ teaspoon monosodium glutamate
½ teaspoon salt
1 pound lean pork, cut in ¾-inch cubes
1 well-beaten egg
½ cup sugar
½ cup vinegar
⅓ cup pineapple juice
¼ cup catsup
1 teaspoon soy sauce
2 tablespoons cornstarch
2 tablespoons water
1 cup pineapple chunks, drained
1 medium green pepper, cut in ½-inch pieces

Combine flour, monosodium glutamate, and salt. Dip pork cubes in beaten egg and then in flour mixture; coat well. Fry pork in deep, hot fat (360°) for 6 to 8 minutes or until browned and done. Remove and drain pork on paper towels and keep warm.

In a wok or deep skillet combine sugar, vinegar, pineapple juice, catsup, and soy sauce; bring to boiling. Blend cornstarch into water; gradually stir into sauce. Continue to simmer mixture, stirring constantly until sauce thickens.

Stir the warm deep fat-fried pork cubes, drained pineapple chunks and green pepper pieces into the thickened sauce. Heat mixture through, stirring constantly for about 5 minutes. Serve while hot with steamed rice. Makes 3 to 4 servings.

PORTLAND

London Grill

When you walk down the red carpeted stairs to the London Grill in the Hotel Benson, you find yourself in a restaurant you'll remember for its excellent food and gracious service, presented against a mellow background of memorabilia from Old England. Pictured at the left is a sample of the lush abundance on the menu: On the silver platter are Breasts of Capon Cordon Bleu; in the center are Medallions of Veal Oscar, and at right is Crab Salad in an Abalone Shell. The desserts are Coupe Trocadero, Black Forest Cake; mugs hold Coffee Wellington.

MEDALLIONS OF VEAL OSCAR

1½ pounds veal tenderloin, well trimmed
¼ cup all-purpose flour
¾ teaspoon salt
Dash pepper
12 ounces fresh crab legs, shelled
2 tablespoons all-purpose flour
1 well beaten egg
½ cup soft bread crumbs
¼ cup butter or margarine
½ cup sauterne
1 cup Bearnaise Sauce

Cut tenderloin into 9 pieces. Flatten slightly with a mallet. Combine ¼ cup flour, salt and pepper; coat pieces of veal. Dip crab meat in 2 tablespoons flour, then in beaten egg, and finally in bread crumbs. Set aside.

Preheat electric skillet to 300°. Fry veal in 2 *tablespoons* of the butter till golden brown, about 10 minutes. Remove to warm platter. Splash hot skillet with sauterne; simmer 1 minute and pour over veal. Place veal uncovered in a low oven to keep warm. Prepare Bearnaise Sauce and keep warm.

In another skillet fry crab in remaining 2 tablespoons butter till brown, about 5 minutes. Remove from heat; keep warm. To assemble; place one heaping teaspoon Bearnaise Sauce over each piece of veal; top with fried crab meat. Pass additional Bearnaise Sauce. Makes 4 to 6 servings.

Note: If fresh crab legs or crab meat are not available use one 6-ounce package frozen king crab meat, thawed.

BREAST OF CAPON CORDON BLEU

1 capon breast, split in half
2 1-ounce slices Swiss cheese
2 1-ounce slices boneless smoked ham
2 tablespoons all-purpose flour
1 well-beaten egg
½ cup soft bread crumbs

Remove capon skin and bones except for wing bone. Remove fillet (loose meat part of inner side of breast). Flatten breast and fillet around wing bone to ⅛ inch. Cut *each* slice cheese and ham into 3 triangular pieces. Lay one piece of ham over one large piece of breast. Top with 3 cheese and 2 ham triangles. Place fillet over filling; overlap edges of breast; pound to seal. Wrap; freeze 15 minutes. Dip meat in flour, egg, and crumbs. Brown in butter in a skillet. Bake at 375° 15 to 20 minutes.

CRAB FILLED ABALONE SHELL

Combine 1 cup cooked crab meat, 1 tablespoon diced celery, 1 tablespoon mayonnaise, 1 teaspoon prepared horseradish, ½ teaspoon lemon juice and salt and pepper to taste. Line an abalone shell with lettuce; fill with crab salad. Makes 1 serving.

COUPE TROCADERO

Combine four 1-ounce squares semisweet chocolate and ¼ cup light cream in top of double boiler; stir over *hot, not boiling* water till chocolate melts. Remove from heat; add 2 to 3 drops orange extract. Spoon ¼ cup into bottom of 4 individual coupe glasses. Chill. To serve top with a small scoop *each* of mint, strawberry, and vanilla ice cream; place a tangerine section between each. Top with whipped cream. Makes 4 servings.

COFFEE WELLINGTON

Blend ½ cup whipping cream and ¼ teaspoon instant coffee; whip to stiff peaks. In each of 6 individual cups place 2 teaspoons coconut syrup; add ½ cup hot coffee and stir till syrup dissolves. Add 2 tablespoons light dry rum. Top with whipped cream.

BLACK FOREST CAKE

Beat 2 egg whites to soft peaks. Beat in ½ cup sugar, beating to stiff peaks. Sift together 1 cup sugar, 1¾ cups sifted cake flour, ¾ teaspoon soda, and 1 teaspoon salt. Add ⅓ cup salad oil and ½ cup milk; beat 1 minute at medium speed on mixer. Scrape bowl constantly. Add ½ cup milk, 2 egg yolks, and two 1-ounce squares melted and cooled unsweetened chocolate. Beat 1 minute longer, scraping bowl frequently. Fold in egg whites. Pour into two paper-lined 9x1½-inch cake pans. Bake in 350° oven 30 to 35 minutes. Cool; split each layer making 4 thin layers. Set aside.

Cherry Filling: Combine 2½ cups drained red sour cherries, ½ cup port, 1 tablespoon kirsch, and 3 drops almond extract. Chill 3 to 4 hours or overnight. Drain thoroughly.

Chocolate Mousse: Combine three 1-ounce squares semisweet chocolate and 3 tablespoons kirsch in top of double boiler; stir over *hot, not boiling* water till chocolate melts and mixture is smooth. Slowly stir into 1 well beaten egg. Whip 1 cup whipping cream and 2 tablespoons sugar; fold into chocolate. Chill 2 hours.

Butter Frosting: Cream ⅓ cup butter; blend in 2 cups sifted confectioners' sugar. Beat in 2 egg yolks and 1 teaspoon vanilla. Blend in 2 cups sifted confectioners' sugar. Add 1½ tablespoons light cream to make of spreading consistency. Chill 30 minutes.

To assemble: Spread ½ cup Butter Frosting on the cut side of a cake layer. With remaining frosting, form a ridge ½ inch wide and ¾ inch high around outside edge; make another ridge 2 inches from outside edge. Chill 30 minutes. Fill space between ridges with Cherry Filling. Spread second layer with Chocolate Mousse and place atop first. Chill 30 minutes. Whip 2 cups whipping cream with 2 tablespoons sugar and 1 teaspoon vanilla. Spread third layer with 1½ *cups* whipped cream and place atop second layer. Top with fourth layer. Reserve ¼ cup whipped cream; frost sides with remainder. Garnish with sweet cooking chocolate curls; sift confectioners' sugar over top. Place 9 dollops of whipped cream atop; center each with a cherry. Chill 2 hours.

SAN FRANCISCO

Ernie's

Ernie's is a very old and attractive restaurant decorated in veritable Victorian style. The claret brocaded wall covering is emphasized by the claret velvet and velveteen in the furnishings. In keeping with great days of the past, heavy crystal chandeliers once used in old Victorian mansions adorn the dining room.

The cuisine is a blend of both the Italian and French schools. Because of the Italian background of the owners and the chef, guests do well when they start dinner with a sampling of the Italian food. A recommended finale is Crepes Ambrosia, a flavorful combination of delicate crepes and ice cream topped with a sauce of fresh strawberries and fruit-flavored liqueurs.

CREPES AMBROSIA

Combine ½ cup sifted all-purpose flour, 2 eggs, 1½ tablespoons sugar, ¾ cup milk, dash salt, and 3 drops vanilla; beat with a rotary beater till smooth. Refrigerate several hours to let thicken a little.

Heat a heavy 6-inch skillet till a drop of water will dance on it. Then grease lightly and pour in 2 tablespoons batter. Lift skillet off heat and tilt from side to side till batter covers bottom evenly. Cook till underside of crepe is lightly browned; the cooking should take only seconds. Cook on one side only. Repeat with remaining batter using 2 tablespoons batter for each crepe. Keep warm.

Mash 2 cups cleaned and hulled fresh strawberries in a chafing dish over flame, or in a 9-inch skillet over low heat. Add 2 tablespoons sugar, ¼ cup kirsch, and ¼ cup orange liqueur; heat just to boiling. Stir and set aflame. Simmer crepes uncovered in the mixture for 3 minutes.

Place one scoop of vanilla ice cream in each of 10 dessert dishes; surround the ice cream with 2 cups cleaned and hulled fresh strawberries. Place a crepe over each serving of ice cream and strawberries; top with some of the strawberry mixture from the chafing dish. Makes 10 servings.

Choose from this pyramid of pancake delights! On top are Super Strawberry Pancakes—each delectable, lacy-edged cake filled with fresh juicy berries. In the center, a circle of Blueberry Pancakes teamed with fluffy whipped orange butter. And last, a plate of delicious, dessert-size Chocolate Pancakes topped with a mountain of sweetened whipped cream and a shower of chocolate shot.

HOST

SAN FRANCISCO

Pancake Palace

With 14 varieties of pancakes from which to choose, you feel like royalty at the Pancake Palace in San Francisco's International Airport. Here, pancakes are perfection—light, airy, hot, and dressed up with your choice of rich sauces, luscious butters, and syrups to please every fancy. Travelers are not the only ones who enjoy the specialties of the Pancake Palace. On Sundays families gather for brunch, and at noon men talk shop over stacks of buckwheats.

SUPER STRAWBERRY PANCAKES

2 slightly beaten eggs
1 cup light cream
½ cup sifted all-purpose flour
1½ teaspoons sugar
¼ teaspoon salt
2 10-ounce packages frozen strawberries, thawed and drained

Combine eggs and cream. Sift flour, sugar, and salt into liquid ingredients; beat smooth. Let stand at least 2 hours so batter thickens and cakes will hold shape on griddle. Beat batter up again; bake on hot, lightly buttered griddle, using 2 tablespoons batter for each. Brown both sides. Roll cakes; place on ovenproof platter. Cover and keep warm in slow oven (300°). To serve, unroll; fill each with spoonful strawberries; roll up. Arrange 3 cakes for a serving. Sift confectioners' sugar over; center with puff of whipped cream and a whole berry.

BLUEBERRY PANCAKES

2 cups sifted all-purpose flour
1 teaspoon *each* salt and soda
2 tablespoons sugar
2 slightly beaten eggs
2 cups buttermilk
2 tablespoons butter, melted
1 1-pound can blueberries, drained

Sift together dry ingredients. Add remaining ingredients, except berries; stir just till moistened. Add ⅔ cup drained berries. Bake on hot, lightly greased griddle; use ¼ cup batter for each. Turn once. Arrange cakes in circle on plates; sift confectioners' sugar over. Center with whipped orange butter; sprinkle with remaining blueberries.

Chocolate Pancakes: Omit sugar and berries from above recipe; add ⅔ cup canned chocolate syrup with liquid ingredients. Arrange cakes in circle; center with whipped cream; sprinkle top with chocolate shot. Makes 2 dozen brunch or dessert hot cakes.

YOSEMITE NATIONAL PARK

The Ahwahnee

From the floor of Yosemite Valley to the wilderness of the high Sierras, Yosemite National Park in California offers a year-round carefree atmosphere of outdoor adventure. In the winter season, guests skate and ski in the exhilarating mountain air. Warmer weather brings swimming, fishing, golf, tennis, as well as educational hikes through a living textbook of nature. Trained guides, under the direction of the National Park Service, are available to give information regarding the flora and fauna, geology, and history of the park.

The Golden Macaroni Salad shown in the foreground of the picture at left is a cheese-flavored dish hearty enough to appease the most voracious outdoor appetite. Also pictured as served at Ahwahnee are California salad bowl, Ahwahnee tenderloin tips with French-fried potato balls, and a velvety devil's food cake.

GOLDEN MACARONI SALAD

1 to 1½ teaspoons yellow food coloring
2 cups ditalini*
6 hard-cooked eggs
¾ cup diced green pepper
¼ cup diced pimiento
½ cup diced sharp Cheddar cheese
2 teaspoons prepared mustard
2 teaspoons salt
½ cup finely chopped onion
Mayonnaise to moisten

Add food coloring to boiling salted water; add ditalini or elbow macaroni and cook till tender. Rinse in cold water; drain.

Sieve the egg yolks and set aside. Chop the egg whites and combine with drained macaroni and remaining ingredients; mix well. Chill thoroughly. To serve, sprinkle the sieved egg yolks over top of the salad; garnish edges with fresh parsley sprigs, if desired. Makes 6 to 8 servings.

*Salad macaroni; or you can use one 7-ounce package elbow macaroni.

NUT TREE

The Nut Tree

Western food at its best is the style at The Nut Tree. Family-type folks on vacation or holiday jaunts welcome this famous countryside stopping-off place between Sacramento and San Francisco. For snacking, Hawaiian Pineapple, Central American Style is a cooling refresher. If it's lunch time, a big fruit, vegetable, or sea food salad such as one of those pictured may hit the spot.

Back of this picture-perfect food is real family pride. In the early Twenties, Ed and Helen Power set up a fruit stand in the shade of a big walnut tree and sold peaches and figs from their orchard to highway travelers. The walnut tree grew. The orchard grew. The roadside stand grew into a group of shops clustering around a group of dining rooms. Today, the Powers with their two sons and daughter manage the food service that began from that one small fruit stand.

FRESH FRUIT PLATE

Have fruit *well chilled.* Arrange thin papaya slices, apple slices, raw cranberries, orange sections, kumquats, watermelon wedge, pineapple slices, whole tangerine, pink grapefruit sections, banana slices, whole fresh pear (pared), and grape cluster on chilled plate. Center with mound of cottage cheese or sherbet; add slices of warm Waffled Orange Nut Bread and trim with fresh flowers or mint. Pass Marshmallow Dressing.

MARSHMALLOW DRESSING

Combine 1 cup sugar, ⅔ cup light corn syrup, and ½ cup hot water. Heat slowly, stirring till sugar dissolves. Then boil, without stirring, to firm-ball stage (248°). Gradually beat hot syrup into 2 stiffly beaten egg whites. Add dash salt and ¼ teaspoon vanilla. Cool. Fold in ¼ cup mayonnaise and 1 tablespoon grated orange peel. Serve with Fresh Fruit Plate, or Hawaiian Pineapple, Central American Style.

WAFFLED ORANGE NUT BREAD

Peel from 2 large oranges
2¼ cups sifted all-purpose flour
¾ cup sugar
3 teaspoons baking powder
1 teaspoon salt
1 cup chopped California walnuts
2 beaten eggs
1 cup milk
3 tablespoons butter, melted

With sharp knife cut peel from oranges in thin strips; lay several strips together and chop fine—you'll need 1 cup chopped. Sift together dry ingredients; add peel and nuts. Combine eggs, milk, and melted butter; add all at once to dry mixture; stir just till moistened. Pour into greased 9½x5x3-inch loaf pan. Bake at 350° for 55 minutes or till done. Remove from pan; cool. Slice in ½-inch slices. Place unbuttered slices in hot waffle iron; toast till browned in waffled pattern. Serve hot with fruit salad.

HAWAIIAN PINEAPPLE, CENTRAL AMERICAN STYLE

Select a thoroughly ripe fresh pineapple; chill. Follow picture directions below for cutting. Cut off top and bottom of pineapple. With a sharp, sturdy knife, cut around fruit inside shell, first from one end, then the other, leaving a thin but firm wall. Remove the solid cylinder; cut into fairly thin slices, then cut down through the stack, making half slices. Slip the slices back in shell through bottom opening. "Pin" the bottom back in place with toothpicks. Arrange filled shell and spiky top on a tray and serve with Marshmallow Dressing.

CHOCOLATE FUDGE CAKE

¾ cup soft butter or margarine
½ cup cocoa
1½ cups sugar
1 teaspoon vanilla
3 egg yolks
2¼ cups sifted cake flour
3 teaspoons baking powder
1 cup cold water (ice cold if warm room)
3 stiffly beaten egg whites

Beat cocoa into butter. Gradually add sugar, beating till light and fluffy. Add vanilla. Beat in egg yolks one at a time. Sift together flour and baking powder; add to creamed mixture alternately with water, a small amount at a time, beating smooth after each addition. Fold in egg whites. Bake in 2 paper-lined 9x1½-inch round cake pans at 300° for 30 to 35 minutes or till done. Cool 10 minutes; turn out; cool on racks. Frost with Rich Chocolate Icing.

RICH CHOCOLATE ICING

3 egg whites
1½ cups sifted confectioners' sugar
¾ cup soft butter
⅓ cup cocoa
½ teaspoon vanilla
⅓ cup almond halves, toasted

Beat egg whites to soft peaks; gradually add ¾ *cup* of the confectioners' sugar, beating to stiff peaks; set aside. Beat butter till creamy. Combine remaining sugar and cocoa; gradually beat into butter. Fold in vanilla and egg whites till well blended. Frost layers and top of Chocolate Fudge Cake; sprinkle with the almonds.

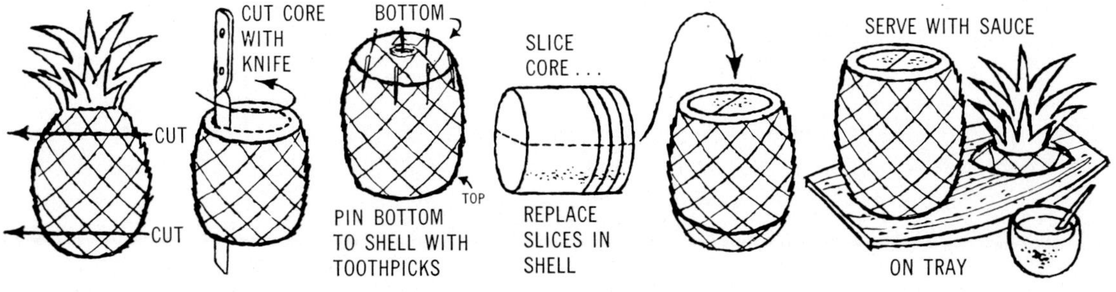

Camellia
ROOM

SAN FRANCISCO

The Fairmont Hotel

To most people who visit or live in San Francisco, it seems to hold enchantment. It is at once sophisticated and worldly, friendly and fun-loving. Residents of San Francisco argue emphatically over which of the many good restaurants serves the best food. Those who prefer a restaurant of long-establishment point to the beautiful Fairmont Hotel, standing atop San Francisco's Nob Hill. One of the specialties served in its festive Camellia Room is Pancake Oscar, an elegant brunch dish of frosted pancakes and hot strawberries.

PANCAKE OSCAR

1 cup sifted all-purpose flour
3 teaspoons baking powder
1 teaspoon sugar
¼ teaspoon salt
1 cup milk
¼ cup light cream
2 tablespoons butter or margarine, melted
1 slightly beaten egg
Melted butter or margarine
Brown sugar
1 pint fresh strawberries, halved
¼ cup sugar
1 recipe Marshmallow Mix

Sift together dry ingredients. Combine milk, cream, butter, and egg; mix well. Add dry ingredients; beat till smooth. (Batter may be prepared and chilled overnight.) Using ¼ cup batter for each pancake, bake on a lightly greased, hot griddle. Spread melted butter over cakes; sprinkle each with 1 teaspoon brown sugar. Stack pancakes; keep warm. Combine strawberries and sugar; heat to boiling. To serve, cut stacked pancakes in wedges; spoon hot strawberries over top. Pass *Marshmallow Mix:* Blend 1 cup marshmallow creme with 2 tablespoons softened butter or margarine. Fold in ¼ cup whipping cream, whipped. Makes ⅔ cup.

SAN FRANCISCO

Trader Vic's

Mr. Victor J. Bergeron, with the help of Assistant Chan Wong and his excellent staff, offers the best in South Seas cuisine. Trader Vic acquired his recipes in his travels, experimented with them, and made them his own. He has changed Chinese, Javanese, and Tahitian dishes to suit American preference and appetite. While the menu doesn't copy typical foods of the Islands, it is slanted to tropical foods capturing the gay spirit of Polynesian feasting.

People from far and near beat a path to the door of Trader Vic's. Name a food, and if it's good, the menu is almost bound to include it. Besides his restaurant home in San Francisco, he operates restaurants in Oakland, Beverly Hills, Washington, D. C., Seattle, Portland, Vancouver, Denver, Scottsdale, Arizona, Chicago, St. Louis, New York, San Juan, Puerto Rico, and in London, England.

Trader Vic has a pet theory: When you have an accumulation of friends, whether they number two or 20, you have ample grounds for a party. And he believes in the easy-does-it approach—an informal *luau* (feast) for instance. At left, Trader adds a torch ginger flower to his *luau* table—it's covered with green *ti* leaves, centered with fruits and blossoms to set off the lavish feast. Up front is a platter of barbecued chicken, Baked Bananas, and sweet potatoes; a bowl of Barbecued Shrimp; serving shells of Island Spareribs and Batter-fried Shrimp. Giant coconuts offer Kona Chicken, a luscious curry; small ones hold punch.

One of Trader Vic's latest innovations is his Hong Kong Club in the San Francisco restaurant. At the request of local businessmen watching their health and weight, Trader Vic developed a whole new line of recipes that have ingeniously preserved good flavor, but have cut down the tally of calories. No health counter this, but a place where the taste runs as high as the fat runs low.

BAKED BANANAS

Bake firm, green-tipped bananas, skins on, in a slow oven (300° to 325°) about 30 minutes or until a fork will pierce them easily. To serve, slit the skin, sprinkle sparingly with salt and lemon or lime juice. Then let guests eat them "on the half shell."

KONA CHICKEN IN A COCONUT

1 teaspoon *each* chopped tomato, chopped green pepper, and chopped pineapple
2 cups Trader Vic's Susu Curry Sauce
1 cup cubed cooked chicken meat
Dash steak sauce
Salt to taste
Seasoned mashed potatoes
Hollandaise Sauce

Mix tomato, pepper, and pineapple well. Add remaining ingredients except potatoes and Hollandaise; heat. Fill a coconut shell (or 1-quart casserole) with this mixture. Decorate the sawed-off section of the husk with hot mashed potato squeezed through a pastry tube. Cover the curry mixture with a tablespoon or so of Hollandaise Sauce. Bake in very hot oven (450°) for 10 to 12 minutes or till potatoes are lightly browned. Serve at the table with steamed rice. Each coconut makes 2 or 3 servings.

TRADER VIC'S SUSU CURRY SAUCE

In a saucepan, saute 1 tablespoon curry powder in 1 tablespoon butter or margarine till nicely browned. Stir in 1 onion, minced, 2 stalks celery, diced, ½ cup sliced mushrooms, and 1 cup diced apple; mix thoroughly. Add ½ cup soup stock; bring mixture to boiling. Stir in 1 cup light cream and 1 cup milk; bring to boiling again. Blend 2 tablespoons cornstarch into 2 tablespoons cold water; add to curry mixture. Cook, stirring constantly, till mixture thickens. Season to taste with monosodium glutamate and salt. Use Susu Curry Sauce for Kona Chicken or, heat cubed chicken or sea food in the sauce and serve over fluffy rice. Makes 3½ cups.

ISLAND SPARERIBS

3 sides small, meaty pork spareribs
¼ cup sugar
1 teaspoon salt
Island Barbecue Sauce

Rub spareribs on both sides with sugar and salt; let stand 2 hours. (Use smoke salt if cooking in the oven.) Brush with Island Barbecue Sauce; let stand at least an hour—preferably longer. Barbecue or hang in Chinese barbecue oven for about an hour. To barbecue in range oven, prepare ribs as above; place meat side up, on rack in shallow pan. Bake in very hot oven (450°) for 15 minutes; pour off fat. Then bake in moderate oven (350°) for about 1 hour or till done, turning ribs and brushing with barbecue sauce a few times. Cut in serving pieces.

ISLAND BARBECUE SAUCE

½ cup soy sauce
½ cup catsup
3 tablespoons brown sugar
1 egg-size gingerroot, grated
1 teaspoon monosodium glutamate

Mix ingredients; let stand overnight before using. Makes about 1 cup sauce.

BATTER-FRIED SHRIMP

2 cups sifted all-purpose flour
½ cup cornstarch
¼ cup white corn meal
½ teaspoon baking powder
1 slightly beaten egg
3 cups water
½ cup milk
5 pounds large raw shrimp, peeled and cleaned

Combine first seven ingredients stirring only until moistened. Take a small amount of batter at a time, in a small bowl; mix in plenty of large raw shrimp so that not too much batter encases them. Have oil very hot, about 400°, for frying. Cook about 3 or 4 minutes. Serve hot with toothpicks for dipping in Sweet and Sour Sauce.

BARBECUED SHRIMP

Let large unpeeled shrimp stand in soy sauce a few minutes. String on skewers. Barbecue over glowing coals 10 minutes or till done, turning a few times. Let diners remove the shells. Serve with Chinese Mustard, Sweet and Sour Sauce, or Red Sauce.

CHINESE MUSTARD

¼ cup dry English mustard
½ teaspoon salt
2 teaspoons salad oil

Stir ¼ cup boiling water into dry mustard. Add salt and oil. If not yellow enough, add some turmeric. Serve with Batter-fried or Barbecued Shrimp. Makes about ⅓ cup.

SWEET AND SOUR SAUCE

1 cup sugar
½ cup distilled vinegar
1 tablespoon chopped green pepper
1 tablespoon chopped pimiento
½ teaspoon salt
2 teaspoons cornstarch
1 teaspoon paprika
Pimiento
Parsley, finely chopped

Mix first 5 ingredients with ½ cup water; simmer 5 minutes. Combine cornstarch and 1 tablespoon cold water; add to hot mixture; cook and stir till sauce thickens. Let cool. Before serving, strain out vegetables. Add paprika, few bits of pimiento, and a little parsley. Makes about 1 cup.

RED SAUCE

3 tablespoons catsup
3 tablespoons chili sauce
3 tablespoons horseradish
1 teaspoon lemon juice
Dash of bottled hot pepper sauce
Salt and pepper to taste

Combine all ingredients thoroughly. For hors d'oeuvres, serve with Batter-fried Shrimp. Makes about ½ cup sauce.

Luau Punch is lovely June Uyeda's greeting to guests. The punch bowl is a big salad-oil can concealed by ti leaves and flowers. Trader Vic's advice for home parties: Improvise your punch bowl—it could be a wooden keg, an ice cake, a hollowed-out log—and formality goes out the window.

LUAU PUNCH

2 10-ounce packages frozen raspberries
3 cups strong black tea
1 quart orange juice
1 cup lime or lemon juice
1 cup crushed pineapple
Sugar to taste

. . .

2 quarts sparkling water, chilled

Let raspberries thaw; sieve or strain, then mix with tea, fruit juices, pineapple, and sugar. Pour over cake of ice in punch bowl. Let chill. Just before serving, add sparkling water. Makes about 4 quarts.

The specialty on the menu at the Holiday House is Roast Long Island Duckling a l'Orange. The tender meat is drenched in a tangy caramelized orange sauce. Speared atop are a round of fresh orange and a maraschino cherry. Golden sweet potatoes and buttered green beans with almonds accompany this dish.

MALIBU

Holiday House

The Holiday House, owned and managed by Mr. Dudley Murphy, is tucked away on a ledge overlooking the blue Pacific in Malibu, California, just 30 miles from Los Angeles. Diners enjoy both the view and the tune of the surf splashing against the rocks below. Their specialty is Roast Long Island Duckling a l'Orange Sauce. Other favorites include French onion soup, Eastern beef charcoal broiled, veal scallopini, and lobster from their own "front yard."

ROAST LONG ISLAND DUCKLING A L'ORANGE SAUCE

2 4-pound Long Island ducklings
2 branches celery
2 small carrots
2 small onions, sliced

. . .

1 recipe Orange Sauce

Sprinkle cavity of ducklings with salt and place a celery branch, small carrot, small sliced onion, and pinch of rosemary in cavity of each duckling. Prick ducks to allow fat to escape; truss. Roast uncovered on a rack in a moderate oven (375°) for 1½ hours and then in a hot oven (425°) for 15 minutes or till golden brown and tender.

Carve breast meat and legs from ducklings for serving on plates. Save remaining parts of ducklings to put in Orange Sauce. Serve hot with sauce. Makes 4 servings.

ORANGE SAUCE FOR DUCKLING

Combine 1½ cups orange juice, 1 cup grape juice, ½ cup spiced brown gravy, ¼ cup currant jelly, 2 tablespoons cooking sherry, 1½ tablespoons lemon juice, 1½ tablespoons brown sugar, pinch dry mustard, and dash nutmeg. Add 2 duck carcasses and bring to boiling. Caramelize 2¼ cups sugar, but do not burn; stir in ¼ cup red wine vinegar and add to first mixture. Simmer until clear, about 10 minutes. (Do not overcook, or a burned taste will result due to sugar and jelly).

Just before serving, remove duck carcasses and strain sauce through cheesecloth. Combine 2 tablespoons cornstarch with 2 tablespoons grape juice, stir till smooth; add to sauce, bring to a boil, cook and stir till thick. Heat duck in 450° oven about 10 minutes; pour hot sauce over. Serves 4.

Mr. Perino checks this selection of salad art: Fruit Salad, Perino Salad, chicken-stuffed tomatoes, Fresh Vegetable Salad and Chef's Salad.

FRESH VEGETABLE SALAD

Form a crown of the following chilled, cooked fresh vegetables by alternating them on a bed of shaved lettuce: strips of cauliflower, beet slices, carrot slices, peas, green beans, and zucchini slices rising to a pinnacle made of broccoli. For smart-looking slices of cooked beets and carrots, use a waffle cutter. For drama, snip points on a few romaine leaves and stand them upright around the edge of the bowl. Serve Fresh Vegetable Salad with 1000 Island Dressing.

FRESH FRUIT SALAD

Start with all ingredients and salad bowls well chilled. Base of salad is mound of fresh fruit, or a bed of shaved lettuce. In a bowl, arrange a circle of pink grapefruit sections, then a circle of strawberries alternating with watermelon cubes. Add 2 more circles of figs with centers of halved purple grapes, and crescents of papaya. Garnish with water cress frosted with confectioners' sugar. Serve with Whipped-cream Dressing.

WHIPPED-CREAM DRESSING

1 cup mayonnaise
½ cup whipping cream, whipped
1 tablespoon Bar-le-duc
Paprika

In a mixing bowl, combine mayonnaise, whipped cream, and Bar-le-duc; mix well. Add just enough paprika to give a pink color to the dressing; chill well. Makes about 1½ cups dressing. Serve with Fresh Fruit Salad.

CHEF'S SALAD

Have all ingredients and serving bowls chilled. On bed of shaved lettuce, lay julienne strips of breast of chicken, ham, Swiss cheese, and pickled tongue. (To cut julienne style, slice the foods about ¼ inch thick, then stack several slices; cut all at once in ¼-inch-wide strips.) Chop yolks and whites of hard-cooked eggs separately; trim salad with a band of each, plus a band of snipped chives. Serve with 1000 Island Dressing or your favorite French dressing.

1000 ISLAND DRESSING

1 cup mayonnaise
½ cup catsup
½ green pepper, finely chopped
2 to 3 sweet gherkins, finely chopped
1 tablespoon finely chopped pimiento
2 to 3 tablespoons finely chopped onion

Blend together all ingredients; chill several hours before serving. Serve with Fresh Vegetable Salad, Perino Salad, or Chef's Salad. Makes about 1½ cups dressing.

PERINO'S

LOS ANGELES

Perino's

Perino's in Los Angeles is a haven of Old-World leisure where jangled nerves may be soothed and gourmet hungers assuaged. Mr. Alexander Perino personally administers perfection from the arrival of the first porter in the morning to the departure of the last dinner guest. His energy seems boundless as he manages every aspect of his operation for no less than seven days each week. Since the restaurant's opening in 1930, unswerving quality has been maintained.

Although Mr. Perino cordially greets guests at the door and personally directs them to their tables, he considers his real work to be in the kitchen supervising the food preparation. Often hovering over a many-potted stove, he manages to see and approve every dish that is prepared and served.

Each day the meats, vegetables, and salad greens used in his restaurant are personally selected by Mr. Perino. Only the best can meet his standards of quality. Well-supplied with many more food items, his kitchen is prepared to serve almost any individual preference in food. However, Mr. Perino does draw the line on one product of modern food processing. Frozen foods are never used in the restaurant—if food items can't be purchased fresh, he won't serve them.

PERINO SALAD

Chill all salad ingredients, as well as the serving dishes. For each salad, fan out slices of one half avocado over a bed of hearts of romaine. For the handsome slices as shown in the picture at left: Cut a nice, ripe avocado in half lengthwise. Remove seed and strip off peel. Lay the avocado halves flat side down and slice crosswise.

Flank the fanned avocado slices with thick wedges of peeled beefsteak tomatoes and border with large cooked shrimp, cut in half lengthwise. Garnish avocado slices with a whole shrimp and a ribbon of pimiento. Serve with 1000 Island Dressing.

HOLLYWOOD

Scandia

By all Viking standards, Scandia in Hollywood (right on fabulous Sunset Boulevard) matches the best in Copenhagen or Stockholm. Comfortable, friendly, and spacious in an Old World way, Scandia shuns the standardized smorgasbord offered in many restaurants in favor of original Scandinavian-style dishes.

At left the specialties shown are Cold Cucumber Soup (top right), Danish Apple Cake, Cucumber Salad, Salmon in Aspic, and Lobster Tails Maison. The Danish motif appears throughout Scandia in china, napery, and glassware.

LOBSTER TAILS MAISON

8 small Danish lobster tails (or medium-size shrimp), cut in thirds
2 tablespoons butter or margarine
2 teaspoons chopped shallots
2 tablespoons lemon juice
4 drops bottled hot pepper sauce
Dash salt
1 teaspoon bottled steak sauce
½ cup white wine
1 cup whipping cream
1 tablespoon soft butter or margarine
2 tablespoons all-purpose flour
2 teaspoons chopped chives
½ cup Hollandaise Sauce
¼ cup whipping cream, whipped
Dash monosodium glutamate
Green grapes

In heavy skillet, brown lobster tails in butter. Add shallots; cook till tender, but not brown. Add next 6 ingredients; heat to boiling. Combine 1 tablespoon butter and 2 tablespoons flour; add to sauce. Add chives. Return sauce to boiling; simmer 2 to 3 minutes. Pour ¼ cup of the sauce in an individual casserole dish; arrange 4 pieces lobster along the outside edge. Blend together Hollandaise, whipped cream, and monosodium glutamate. Spread 2 tablespoons over each filled dish. Garnish with green grapes. Broil 4 inches from heat for about 1 minute; serve immediately. Makes 6 servings.

DANISH APPLE CAKE

2 1-pound 4-ounce cans (about 6 cups) sliced apples
1 cup sugar
1 tablespoon lemon juice
4 cups fine macaroon crumbs (about 1 pound macaroons)
½ cup butter or margarine, melted
1 10-ounce jar (about 1 cup) currant jelly

In a saucepan, combine apples, sugar and lemon juice; simmer 5 minutes. Drain mixture (do not use liquid) and sieve apples. Combine macaroon crumbs and butter. Lightly press 2 cups of the crumb mixture on bottom of 7-inch spring-form pan. Top with ½ the sieved apples; spread with ½ *cup* of the currant jelly. Repeat layering with *1 cup* of the crumb mixture, remaining apples and jelly. Sprinkle remaining crumbs on top pressing down lightly. Bake in a moderate oven (350°) for 40 to 45 minutes. Chill overnight. Just before serving, remove from pan. If desired, decorate with whipped cream and toasted sliced almonds.

COLD CUCUMBER SOUP

3 medium cucumbers
½ cup chopped onion
2 tablespoons butter
2 bay leaves
1 tablespoon all-purpose flour
3 cups chicken broth
1 teaspoon salt
1 cup light cream
2 tablespoons lemon juice
Pinch dried dill weed
Sour cream

Pare cucumbers; slice 2 cucumbers. Add chopped onion and cook in butter with bay leaves until tender but not brown. Blend in flour; add broth and salt. Simmer covered for 20 to 30 minutes. Sieve mixture; chill well. Skim off any fat. Scoop out and discard seeds of remaining cucumber. Grate and add to chilled mixture. Add cream, lemon juice, and dill. Serve in chilled cups with a dollop of sour cream stirred in. Sprinkle dill over top for garnish. Makes 6 servings.

CUCUMBER SALAD

1 medium cucumber, peeled and thinly sliced
½ teaspoon salt
⅓ cup sugar
½ cup white vinegar
¼ cup water
Dash white pepper
Finely snipped parsley

Sprinkle sliced cucumber with salt; let stand 30 minutes. Drain and squeeze in hands. Combine sugar, vinegar, water, and pepper; pour over cucumber slices. Sprinkle parsley over top. Chill 30 minutes. Serves 4 to 5.

SALMON IN ASPIC

1 1-pound salmon fillet
1½ cups white wine
¾ cup water
½ cup white vinegar
2 tablespoons chopped onion
4 whole allspice
2 tablespoons sugar
2 bay leaves
1 tablespoon salt
½ teaspoon monosodium glutamate
¼ teaspoon dried dill weed

• • •

1½ envelopes (1½ tablespoons) unflavored gelatin
½ cup cold water
3 stiffly beaten egg whites

Cut salmon into bite-size pieces; combine with next 10 ingredients in a saucepan. Bring just to boiling; reduce heat and simmer 10 minutes; cool. Remove salmon and strain liquid. Soften gelatin in ½ cup cold water and add to cooled liquid; return to saucepan. Spoon beaten egg whites on the surface of liquid. Heat slowly, whisking egg whites back and forth across the center of the pan till liquid boils, about 10 minutes. Remove from heat; let cool 30 minutes.

Strain the liquid through a sieve lined with cheesecloth dampened in cold water. Do not stir. Let gelatin mixture stand till partially set. Gently fold in salmon; turn mixture into a 1-quart mold. Chill till firm.

HOLLYWOOD

Beverly Hills Club

Established in 1928, the Beverly Hills Club has grown to a membership of 2,000. The French Continental theme of its decor is especially appropriate on those special evenings when the menu honors Paris. French Pineapple Tart features apricot-glazed pineapple over a rich custard, held in a nut-trimmed crust.

FRENCH PINEAPPLE TART

Make a pastry shell: Sift together 1 cup sifted all-purpose flour, 1 teaspoon sugar, and ¼ teaspoon salt. Cut in ⅓ cup butter or margarine till mixture resembles coarse crumbs. Knead carefully in a bowl till dough becomes a paste. Stir in 1 tablespoon milk. Place dough on a lightly floured surface and roll to 1/16-inch thickness. Butter an 8x1½-inch round pan; pat dough on bottom and up sides. Cut a round piece of paper to fit the pan. Butter one side of the paper; place butter side down over dough; fill pan with rock salt or navy beans to hold dough in shape. Bake in a slow oven (300°) till lightly browned, about 35 minutes. Cool for a few minutes on a rack; remove rock salt or beans and paper. *Gently* remove crust from pan by inverting *carefully* on a cake rack. Combine ½ cup sugar, ¼ cup all-purpose flour, and ¼ teaspoon salt in a double boiler; gradually stir in 2 cups scalded milk. Cook and stir till the thickness of medium white sauce. Remove from heat. Beat together 4 egg yolks and 2 eggs. Stir a small amount of the hot mixture into eggs; blend into remaining hot mixture. Return to heat and cook over *hot*, not boiling water till thick, stirring constantly. Remove from heat; add 1 teaspoon vanilla. Cool. Fill crust with custard mixture. Decorate top with 10 slices canned pineapple, drained and cut in fourths. Spread with ½ cup apricot jam, sieved. Sprinkle ⅓ cup chopped walnuts around edge. Serves 6 to 8.

FARMERS MARKET
FRUIT AND PRODUCE
LEE AND ANNA PYATT
LEE
FARMERS MARKET
FRUIT & PRODUCE CO.
Grandpa won't Permit handling!

LOS ANGELES

Farmers Market

Enter shoppers' paradise! Nowhere else in the world will you find more beautiful foods than at the Farmers Market in Los Angeles, a trading post of over 150 stalls and supermarkets and places to eat (gift and specialty stores, too). It all began during the Depression when a small group of farmers located produce stalls on an empty field in town to drum up business. Soon, meat dealers and grocers wanted in, and Farmers Market snowballed. As you stroll from booth to booth, the spanking white clapboard buildings may remind you of New England. Many a gourmet swaps recipes with the proprietors who know more than a thing or two about their cooking wares. Now let's visit a few of the food shops.

FAIRFAX GINGER PEACHES
(Pyatt's Fruit and Produce)

½ cup orange juice
2 tablespoons honey
Dash salt
4 cups sliced peeled ripe peaches
2 tablespoons finely chopped candied ginger

Blend orange juice, honey, and salt; add peach slices and candied ginger; mix gently. Cover and chill thoroughly. Spoon into chilled sherbets. Garnish with flaked coconut, additional candied ginger and mint sprigs, if desired. Makes 4 to 5 servings.

WESTERN CHAFING-DISH SALAD
(Pyatt's Fruit and Produce)

Wash 1 pound fresh spinach, discarding stems. Pat leaves dry on paper towels; tear in bite-size pieces into bowl. Add 4 sliced green onions and tops and sprinkle with coarsely ground black pepper. Chill.

At serving time, slowly fry 5 slices diced bacon in a deep chafing dish or electric skillet till crisp-cooked. Add 2 tablespoons wine vinegar, 1 tablespoon lemon juice, 1 teaspoon sugar, ½ teaspoon salt, and spinach; toss till leaves are coated and wilted slightly. Sprinkle 1 coarsely chopped hard-cooked egg over. Makes 4 to 6 servings.

YOGURT DRESSING
(*Boris Juice Bar*)

Combine 1 cup yogurt, 2 tablespoons mayonnaise, 1 teaspoon sugar, dash of lemon juice and pinch of salt; stir well. Keep dressing chilled till ready to serve on fresh fruit salad. Makes about 1 cup dressing.

BRATWURST IM BIER
(*Langston's Sausage*)

Cover 1 pound Bratwurst with cold water; bring to boiling; drain. Brown sausage in 2 tablespoons butter. Add 1 cup beer, 2 bay leaves, 6 peppercorns, and dash salt. Simmer about 5 minutes to reduce liquid.

Remove sausage and strain liquid. Return sausage and strained liquid to pan; add ½ cup beer (or enough to cover sausage), and simmer gently 15 minutes. Blend 1 tablespoon all-purpose flour and 2 tablespoons water to a smooth paste; stir into sauce. Cook, stirring constantly till mixture thickens. Serve sausage in a bowl with the sauce poured over. Makes 4 servings.

MR. MAGEE'S TOMATO ASPIC
(*Magee's*)

2 envelopes (2 tablespoons) unflavored gelatin
½ cup cold water
2½ cups tomato juice
1 6-ounce can (⅔ cup) tomato paste
2 tablespoons tarragon vinegar
1 large onion, minced
1 tablespoon finely chopped green pepper
1 teaspoon salt
Dash coarsely cracked pepper
1 bay leaf
Grated peel from ½ lemon
Juice from ½ lemon
2 sprigs fresh sweet basil

Soften gelatin in cold water. Combine next 8 ingredients; bring to boiling. Add softened gelatin to hot mixture and stir to dissolve. Add remaining ingredients; stir well. Remove bay leaf and basil. Pour into a 5½-cup ring mold; chill till firm. Unmold on greens and serve with mayonnaise.

PATSY'S PIZZA
(*Patsy D'Amore's*)

1 package active dry yeast
1 cup warm water
3½ cups sifted all-purpose flour
1 tablespoon olive oil
1 teaspoon salt
2 tablespoons olive oil
1 pound Italian sausage
2 fresh tomatoes, peeled and sliced thin
1 6-ounce package Mozzarella cheese, *sliced thin* and cut in pieces
1 6-ounce can (⅔ cup) tomato paste
2 cloves garlic, minced
2 tablespoons crushed oregano
1 tablespoon dry parsley flakes
Salt
Freshly ground coarse pepper
About ¼ cup olive oil
¼ cup grated Romano or Parmesan cheese

Soften yeast in water. Beat in 1½ *cups flour;* mix in 1 *tablespoon* olive oil and 1 teaspoon salt. Stir in remaining flour. Knead on lightly floured surface till smooth and elastic, about 12 minutes. (Dough will be very firm.) Place in lightly greased bowl, turning once to grease surface. Cover; let rise till more than double, about 1½ hours. (Dough will have a yeasty odor.) Punch down, cover and refrigerate till cold.

Cut dough in 2 parts. On floured surface, roll each in a 12-inch circle. Place on greased baking sheets or 12-inch pizza pans, turning edge of dough up slightly. Gash bottom about every 2 inches to prevent bubbles. Brush each crust with 1 tablespoon olive oil.

Break sausage in small bits in skillet; fry slowly till lightly browned, about 10 minutes, stirring occasionally. Drain. Place a layer of tomato slices on pizza-dough circles; cover with *half* the Mozzarella cheese. Combine tomato paste and garlic, mixing well; spread over cheese. Sprinkle with seasonings. Drizzle with some of the olive oil. Top with sausage, then remaining Mozzarella. Sprinkle with Romano or Parmesan cheese; drizzle with remaining olive oil. Dash with salt and pepper. Bake in 425° oven 20 minutes or till crust is done. Makes 2.

MEDITERRANIA

LOS ANGELES

Mediterrania

Although the look of the new Mediterrania is reminiscent of no specific locale, its fanciful decorative concept reflects the casual charm, the warmth, the color and the romance of the sun-drenched countries that border on the Mediterranean. The dishes served are not truly Spanish, French, or Italian—yet they suggest, in their flavor, appeal, and service, the influence of the countries that inspired them.

Granada Salad, a potpourri of crisp greens and vegetables served with a Spanish dressing is a favorite at this LaCienega Boulevard oasis. An accompaniment to several of their entrees is Rice Valencia—a combination of onion, green pepper, fresh mushrooms, garlic, rice and herbs cooked in a chicken broth. From their wine cellar you may choose the right wine to complement your dinner, or if you prefer, they'll draw dry Burgundy or white Chablis from their own casks.

RICE VALENCIA

½ cup chopped onion
½ cup chopped green pepper
¾ cup coarsely chopped fresh mushrooms
1 clove garlic, minced
½ cup butter or margarine
1 teaspoon paprika
3 cups long-grain rice
4½ cups chicken broth
½ cup peas
3 teaspoons salt
1 teaspoon monosodium glutamate
1 tablespoon chopped pimiento

Cook chopped onion, green pepper, fresh mushrooms, and garlic in ¼ *cup* butter or margarine until tender but not brown. Blend in paprika and rice. Add chicken broth, peas, salt and monosodium glutamate. Bring mixture to a boil; remove from heat and turn into a 2½-quart casserole.

Bake in a moderate oven (350°) for about 25 to 30 minutes or until rice is fluffy and tender. Remove from oven and add 1 tablespoon chopped pimiento and dot with remaining ¼ *cup* butter or margarine. Fluff rice lightly with a fork. Serve while hot. Makes 10 to 12 servings.

It *is* the Gay '90s in every detail at the Ice Cream Parlor on Main Street, U.S.A. in Disneyland. Here the treats of yesteryear are recaptured in a cherry soda or mug of cocoa. Colossal sundaes are happy ideas from the ice-cream bar. Service comes from an attractive girl in striped Gay '90s costume.

ANAHEIM

Disneyland

Everyone has heard about Disneyland, has either been there himself or knows someone who has visited there. It's a place where fairy tales, folklore, and stories of tomorrow have assumed life-size reality. Each year many people walk through this huge park taking a jungle safari here or a rocket trip there. Although there's excitement enough to keep visitors alert, tired feet and hearty appetites are inevitable. The restaurants within Disneyland serve many purposes. They present a period of American life or specialize in a well-liked food. On Main Street, U.S.A., the Ice Cream Parlor can perk up customers with just about any combination of ice creams and sauces imaginable. A turn-of-the-century theme marks the Coffee House. Families who want to relax a while and have a complete meal find this a refreshing spot. In the Red Wagon Restaurant, the menu caters both to people who want to "eat and run," and to those who want to relax.

VICTORIAN BANANA SPLIT

Cut a fully ripe banana that is flecked with brown, in half lengthwise, place on sides of ice cream dish. Fill between with a scoop *each* of vanilla, chocolate, and strawberry ice creams. Ladle strawberry *and* marshmallow sauces over vanilla ice cream, chocolate sauce on chocolate ice cream, and crushed pineapple on strawberry ice cream. Flood dish with all four sauces. Top with a dollop of whipped cream and maraschino cherry.

SANTA FE EXPRESS

Fill an ice cream dish with a scoop *each* of vanilla, chocolate, and strawberry ice creams (or a combination of your favorite flavors). Ladle over a variety of ice cream sauces. Cut circles from a fully ripe banana for wheels (see picture), arrange sugar wafers for cowcatcher, and use maraschino cherries for the headlight and caboose. Stack up three regular marshmallows for the smokestack and top with whipped cream smoke.

Gay Nineties Sundae is a thriller of a sundae built in luscious layers. A big spoonful of strawberry sauce is in the bottom, then a scoop of vanilla ice cream, *more* sauce, *more* ice cream, and a steeple of whipped cream and whole fresh strawberries.

Gibson Girl Parfait begins with 3 scoops vanilla ice cream and sundae sauce. The topper of whipped cream, almond bits, and a maraschino cherry towers high, reminiscent of a Gibson Girl pompadour. For marbling, run knife down side, lift up.

Disneyland's Coffee House boasts exact replicas of turn-of-the century furnishings in all their plush elegance. To go with a hospitable cup of coffee, Manager Raul Grisanti recommends their hot-fudge ice-cream cake (below), a favorite with his guests. To make, split wedges of freshly baked sponge cake. Spoon vanilla, chocolate, or pink peppermint ice cream over bottom layer; replace top layer of cake. Spoon Hot Fudge Sauce over all.

HOT FUDGE SAUCE

2 1-ounce squares unsweetened chocolate
⅓ cup water
½ cup sugar
Dash salt
3 tablespoons butter or margarine
¼ teaspoon vanilla

In a small saucepan, combine chocolate and water. Stir over low heat till blended. Add sugar and salt; cook *slowly*, stirring constantly, till sugar dissolves and mixture thickens slightly. Remove from heat; add butter and vanilla, stirring till sauce is smooth. Makes about 1 cup sauce.

LOVER'S DELIGHT SUNDAE

Place a large scoop each of strawberry and vanilla ice cream in an individual serving dish. Top strawberry ice cream with marshmallow topping, and vanilla ice cream with strawberry topping. Sprinkle toasted almond bits over all and spoon a dollop of whipped cream between scoops of ice cream. Perch a maraschino cherry atop the whipped cream. Serve with 2 spoons.

There's nothing like a sirloin-steak sandwich for hungry folks on the go. Broiled meat is propped on toast to catch every drop of juice, and served with crisp French Fries and onion rings.

Red Wagon guests in a hurry to ride the horse-car or play the nickelodeons lunch on Chef's Special Cold Plate. Slices of baked ham, turkey breast, and Swiss cheese are arranged with Potato Salad.

RED WAGON RESTAURANT FRENCH FRIES

Wash and pare several potatoes. Cut potatoes lengthwise in strips. Soak 1 hour in cold water to cover; drain thoroughly between towels. Fry a small amount at a time in deep hot fat (360°) until just light brown. Drain on paper towels. Cool thoroughly. Cover and refrigerate until serving time.

Return potatoes to deep hot fat (375°) for a minute or two until they are crisp and golden brown. Drain on paper towels. Sprinkle with salt; serve at once.

Note: New potatoes burn easily in hot fat and are not suitable for French frying.

COFFEE MOCHA CONTINENTAL

½ cup freshly brewed coffee, chilled
½ cup cocoa (prepared as beverage), chilled
Whipped cream
Dash cinnamon

Place ice cubes in a glass. Fill with chilled coffee and cocoa. Top with whipped cream; sprinkle with cinnamon. Makes 1 serving.

POTATO SALAD

6 medium potatoes

• • •

3 hard-cooked eggs, chopped
1 cup chopped celery
1½ teaspoons salt
¼ teaspoon paprika

• • •

¼ cup French dressing
Mayonnaise

Scrub potatoes thoroughly; leave jackets on. Cook whole in boiling, salted water to cover; drain and peel. Cut potatoes in cubes; add chopped eggs, chopped celery, salt, and paprika. Mix in French dressing; chill salad 4 to 6 hours. Before serving, add just enough mayonnaise to moisten salad. Serve with a salad scoop. Makes about 8 servings.

COFFEE HOUSE TUNA ROLL

Split a sesame seed roll in half. Spoon a tuna salad mixture on one half of the roll. On the other half, arrange shredded lettuce and sliced pickles. Top with mayonnaise and a ripe olive garnish. Makes 1 serving.

Inter-Island Resorts

KAILUA-KONA

Kona Inn

On the balmy west coast of the Big Island of Hawaii, this picturesque hotel, one of the Inter-Island Resorts, combines the charm of old Hawaii with modern luxuries. "At the Kona Inn, formality is out; muumuus and aloha shirts are in," says General Manager Herman Mulder. Therefore, guests can shed the cares of a work-a-day world, laze on the sundeck or sandy beach, play a set of tennis, or perhaps even bring a sailfish to gaff!

Kona Inn is a mecca for sports fishermen. But you don't have to be an expert angler to have the thrill of deep-sea fishing. Even a beginner can charter a boat, complete with skipper, and spend the day trolling off the Kona coast where some of the biggest game fish in the world are caught. You might land a marlin (sailfish), an ahi (tuna) or a mahimahi (dolphin). Whatever it is, you can be sure it will be greeted with proper fanfare of bell-ringing and an appreciative audience at the weigh-in station on the lawn of the Inn.

The dining room at Kona Inn is open to the sea, and in the evening, Kailua Bay makes a shimmering soft backdrop for native dancers. The menu of the Inn reflects its sea and sport with gourmet items such as South Pacific mahimahi steak, broiled and served with toasted macadamia-nut butter, and with island favorites such as teriyaki and lamb curry. They also serve the best in roast prime ribs, broiled steaks, and baked hams for those Mainlanders (Haoles) who won't venture forth in eating as they do in travel.

Executive Chef Lee Siebenthaler shares his recipe for Double Fruit-glazed Pork Chops (at left), sensational with or without the orchids. The meat takes on a tart-sweet flavor and high gloss. Cartwheels of orange, lemon, and lime give Island drama with little effort indeed.

From left, against the blue of Kailua Bay: Mauna Loa Parfaits rich with chocolate, Kona Sunset with fresh coconut, Passion Fruit Punch made from the fruits of the Islands, Bananas in Nectar, and Butter Crisp Cookies that fairly melt in your mouth—just perfect with ice cream sundaes and parfaits.

DOUBLE FRUIT-GLAZED PORK CHOPS

6 6- to 8-ounce double-rib pork chops
Salt
Pepper

• • •

2 cups brown sugar
½ cup unsweetened pineapple juice
½ cup honey
2 teaspoons dry mustard
6 whole cloves
12 whole coriander seeds, crushed

Brown chops in skillet; season with salt and pepper, then place in shallow baking pan. Combine remaining ingredients for sauce, and spoon about 3 tablespoons over each chop. Bake uncovered at 350° for 1¼ hours or till done, basting now and then with rest of sauce. With toothpick, peg a slice *each* of orange, lemon, and lime on every chop, top with maraschino cherry; baste fruit with sauce and bake 10 minutes longer. To serve, arrange the chops on leaf-lined platter with Honeyed Bananas. Makes 6 servings.

HONEYED BANANAS

Peel 6 bananas; dip in lemon juice. Melt 2 tablespoons butter in skillet; stir in ¼ cup honey. Add bananas, cook over low heat, turning gently, until hot and glazed. Don't overcook—takes only a few minutes.

BUTTER CRISP COOKIES

⅓ cup butter or margarine
¼ cup sugar
1 egg yolk
¼ teaspoon almond extract
Dash salt
1 cup minus 2 tablespoons sifted all-purpose flour

Thoroughly cream butter and sugar. Add next 3 ingredients; beat well. Gradually add flour, mixing till smooth. (Don't chill.) Force dough through cooky press onto ungreased baking sheet. Bake at 375° for 8 to 10 minutes or till golden brown. Makes about 3 dozen tea-size cookies.

MAUNA LOA PARFAITS

Start each parfait with a large spoonful of chocolate syrup in the bottom of a chilled parfait glass. Add 3 small scoops of chocolate ice cream and then another large spoonful of the chocolate syrup.

To get a pretty marbled effect as in the picture, run a knife down the side of the glass, then lift it up. To serve, top parfaits with generous dollop of whipped cream and trim with toasted macadamia nuts.

KONA SUNSET

For each serving, roll a large scoop of vanilla ice cream in fresh grated or flaked coconut; coat well. Then place ice cream in a chilled sherbet dish.

Tint coconut syrup with a few drops of yellow food coloring, then drizzle the syrup over coconut-coated ice cream. Top each serving with a mandarin-orange section and maraschino cherry. Trim each with two Butter Crisp Cookies.

PASSION FRUIT PUNCH

Combine equal amounts of canned passion fruit (lilikoi) juice, guava or peach nectar, and unsweetened pineapple juice. Add enough maraschino-cherry syrup or grenadine to tint punch pink.

Pour the punch over ice cubes. Garnish each glass of punch with a maraschino cherry and a halved orange slice slipped on a glass stirrer; also tuck in a pineapple spear and sprig of fresh mint.

BANANAS IN NECTAR

To keep bananas pretty and bright, slice them into chilled orange, grapefruit, or pineapple juice and drain.

Then, fill chilled sherbet dishes with the sliced bananas. Add enough frosty-cold guava, papaya, or apricot nectar to each sherbet to cover the slices.

Garnish each serving with mandarin-orange sections, maraschino cherry, and sprig of mint. Serve bananas this way as an appetizer or light dessert.

HAWAIIAN WALDORF SALAD

1 cup crushed pineapple (1 9-ounce can)

• • •

½ cup golden seedless raisins

• • •

2 cups fresh or frozen pineapple chunks, *well* drained
2 cups diced celery

• • •

1 cup mayonnaise

Drain the crushed pineapple *well*, reserving syrup. Add raisins to the reserved syrup and heat just to boiling. Remove from heat and let stand for 10 minutes to plump raisins, then drain. Mix pineapple chunks, diced celery, and drained raisins. Combine the crushed pineapple with the mayonnaise; add to raisin and pineapple mixture and toss lightly. Chill salad well. To serve, arrange in lettuce-lined bowl. For trim, roll the edges of 1 or 2 pineapple rings in snipped parsley; add maraschino cherries and parsley sprigs. Makes 6 servings.

PAPAYA KAMEHAMEHA

Dice chilled ripe papaya, banana, apple, and pineapple into chilled pineapple juice; drain. Pile drained fruits into papaya halves. Garnish with mandarin oranges, maraschino cherries, and sprigs of fresh mint. Serve with Banana Creme Dressing.

BANANA CREME DRESSING

3 fully ripe bananas
2 tablespoons brown sugar
2 tablespoons honey or coconut syrup

• • •

1 cup whipping cream, whipped

Peel the bananas. Then, mash peeled bananas with brown sugar and honey until smooth; sieve. Fold the sieved banana mixture into the whipped cream. (Or fold the banana mixture into prepared dessert topping—use one 2-ounce package dessert-topping mix.) Serve with Papaya Kamehameha or try spooning it over any melon and pineapple salad. Makes 3 cups dressing.

KAUAI

Coco Palms

With its lava-rock setting, white sand beaches, and Hawaiian-style thatched roof cottages, Coco Palms is one of the Island Holidays resort hotels. Here, amidst tropical grandeur, you can take a dip in the ocean or in the Queen's Bath pool, golf or fish, sail down the flower-banked lagoon or up the Wailua River to the famous Fern Grotto.

The Coco Palms is built on the island of Kauai, whose shores are steeped in history and legend. This is the place where Kauai's ancient kings held court. The coconut palm grove *is* the royal forest, the largest in the Hawaiian Islands.

At dinner each night, the ancient rituals of the island are re-enacted. Once again the sounds of the Conch Shell and the ancient drum beats are heard as Malo-clad youths call you to a lavish Polynesian feast. Then they run, swinging flares, along the banks of the lagoon and through the palm grove to light 150 torches. A beautiful sight, not soon to be forgotten.

Across from the open dining room of the House of Singing Bamboo is the Ancient Fire Pit (left) supervised by Island-born Chef Jiro Okamoto. Every day of the week a different kind of meat turns on the spits. When a whole carcass of lamb or a whole pig is barbecued, it is stuffed with local herbs. Smoked hams are sprinkled with dark-brown raw sugar and coconut honey for a final glaze. Turkeys filled with macadamia-nut stuffing are basted with coconut milk while rotating over the hot coals. Pictured at left, eight standing-rib roasts of beef barbecue at one time on the mammoth spits. Here Chef Jiro swishes on his sweet-sour Fire-pit Basting Sauce with a ti-leaf brush, while the Kiaw wood gives off its fragrant smoke to the fire-pit roasts.

FIRE-PIT BASTING SAUCE

⅓ cup soy sauce
½ cup salad oil
½ cup wine vinegar
½ cup lemon juice
1 tablespoon grated gingerroot, *or*
  1 teaspoon dry ginger
½ teaspoon monosodium glutamate
¼ teaspoon cracked pepper
2 cloves garlic, crushed

Thoroughly combine all ingredients. Use to baste beef or lamb roasts.

SESAME DRESSING

⅔ cup sugar
½ teaspoon salt
¼ teaspoon dry mustard
¼ teaspoon paprika
¼ teaspoon bottled hot pepper sauce
½ teaspoon Worcestershire sauce
2 tablespoons minced onion

• • •

1 cup salad oil
⅓ cup vinegar
¼ cup sesame seed, toasted

Mix first 7 ingredients. Gradually add oil, beating constantly. Add vinegar slowly, mixing well. Chill. Add sesame seeds just before serving. Delicious with fruits with gentle flavor such as melons, papayas, or pears. Makes about 1¾ cups dressing.

BLUE-CHEESE DRESSING

½ cup dairy sour cream
¼ cup mayonnaise
Dash salt

• • •

¼ cup crumbled blue cheese

Thoroughly blend sour cream, mayonnaise, and salt. Stir in crumbled blue cheese. Chill well. Serve with fresh fruit. Makes 1 cup.

Salad luncheon is served buffet-style alongside the lagoon. Guests shower assorted fruits with fresh coconut and then take their choice of delicious fruit dressings—all specialties of the Coco Palms.

ORANGE FRENCH DRESSING

½ 6-ounce can (⅓ cup) frozen orange-juice concentrate
⅔ cup salad oil
1 tablespoon vinegar
¼ cup sugar
¼ teaspoon salt
¼ teaspoon dry mustard
Dash bottled hot pepper sauce

Combine all ingredients in a jar. Cover and shake until very well mixed. Chill thoroughly. Serve over banana or pineapple salads. Makes about 1⅓ cups dressing.

PASSION-FRUIT CHIFFON PIE

¼ cup sugar
Dash salt
1 envelope (1 tablespoon) unflavored gelatin
1 cup canned passion-fruit (lilikoi) nectar
4 slightly beaten egg yolks
1 tablespoon lemon juice

• • •

4 egg whites
½ cup sugar

• • •

1 9-inch baked pastry shell
1 cup whipping cream, whipped and sweetened

Thoroughly combine ¼ cup sugar, the salt, and gelatin. Stir in passion-fruit nectar. Heat, stirring constantly, until gelatin dissolves. Stir small amount hot mixture into egg yolks; return to hot mixture. Cook, stirring constantly, until mixture thickens slightly. Remove from heat and add lemon juice. Cool, stirring often, until mixture is partially set.

Beat egg whites until stiff but not dry; gradually add ½ cup sugar, beating until soft peaks form. Gently fold passion-fruit mixture into beaten egg whites, then pile into cooled pastry shell. Chill until firm. To serve, spread with sweetened whipped cream and garnish with sliced bananas or thin slices of fresh lilikoi, if desired.

ISLAND NUT BANANAS

Peel and slice all-yellow or fully ripe bananas. Dip slices in mixture of equal parts honey and lime juice, then sprinkle with chopped macadamia nuts.

COCONUT HOT CAKES WITH KAUAIIAN SAUSAGE

2 cups sifted all-purpose flour
4 teaspoons baking powder
Dash salt

• • •

2 beaten eggs
2 cups milk
¼ cup butter or margarine, melted

• • •

Fresh Grated Coconut

• • •

10 cooked smoked sausage links

Sift together the flour, baking powder, and dash salt. Combine beaten eggs, milk, and ¼ cup melted butter; add to dry ingredients, stirring just until flour is moistened. (Batter will be lumpy.)

Bake cakes on hot griddle, (sprinkle griddle with few drops of water—they'll dance on surface when temperature is right). Turn cakes only once, when top is bubbly and a few bubbles have broken.

Spread each warm cake with honey or coconut syrup, then rcll up. Place three cakes on a mound of grated or flaked coconut for each serving, then drizzle with melted butter. Top each cake with a butter pat and then with sizzling hot sausage links (two per serving). Offer guava jelly, papaya jam, poha jelly, and warm maple syrup. Makes 15 hot cakes or 5 servings.

FRESH GRATED COCONUT

Crack coconut, break off shell. Use vegetable parer or sharp paring knife to remove the brown skin.

Cut coconut in cubes and grate in an electric blender, following manufacturer's directions. Or put pieces of coconut through shredder attachment of an electric mixer. Or use a hand shredder.

Index

D

E-F

G-H

I-J-K

L-M

N-O-P

R-S

T

V-W

Y-Z

By Restaurants